AN APPROACH TO TOWN PLANNING

PUBLICATIONS OF THE INSTITUTE OF SOCIAL STUDIES

PAPERBACK SERIES

III

PROCUL CERNENS

CLARIUS OBSERVAT

INTERNATIONAAL INSTITUUT
VOOR SOCIALE STUDIËN - 'S GRAVENHAGE
1971

AN APPROACH TO TOWN PLANNING

by

F. B. GILLIE

1971
MOUTON
THE HAGUE · PARIS

PRINTED IN THE NETHERLANDS BY GEUZE & CO DORDRECHT

PREFACE

This book originated from the difficulty in finding published material which expounded the elements of town planning for young men studying that subject in developing countries. Some of the available books were good in themselves, but almost none were suitable for this particular purpose. The most frequent difficulty was that available books discussed town planning in terms of the problem as it existed in one western country, so that they failed to bring out the nature of the fundamental problems as opposed to the form which they happened to take in particular circumstances. Little attempt had been made to distil the common elements of the problems which occur very widely.

Hitherto, moreover, writers have insufficiently emphasised that town planning involves far more than preparing a single plan for the future of a town. To be fully understood it must be thought of as a continuing process of managing growth and change. Towns are continually changing (often because they are continually growing) so that the communal organisation and the relations between individual interests need to be constantly adjusted. All the research, mapping and designing that are employed in town planning are only valuable if they assist the day-by-day process of making the town a convenient and useful place in the light of changing demands. But, though a town is constantly changing, the changes are normally slow and the adjustments to meet them have to be gradual. This emphasises the problem of looking ahead and judging what is going to happen and how fast the new developments will come. This book therefore lays stress on the need to understand the forces at work in towns and the way in which they operate.

A number of the most famous books about town planning, e.g. those of Le Corbusier, are expositions of a particular view as to what the city of the future should be like. Some of these have made valuable contributions to lively and intelligent thinking about towns, but their treatment of the subject has little to do with the detailed problems that have to be handled day by day. Doubtless the authors of these books often recognised this and consciously tried to jolt current thinking out of an excessive preoccupation with everyday problems. On the other hand, the best of such authors would also recognise that, however magnificent or revolutionary the ideal to which the town planner is working, he must nevertheless be able to cope efficiently with day-to-day business. A principal aim of the present book is to demonstrate what the essence of the day-to-day business is and what is necessary for its sound organisation. The book contends that the problems discussed in it must always be dealt with, whatever the urban ideal or the nature of the government of the country concerned. On the other hand, no attempt is made to go into full technical detail. The aim is to equip the student with a good understanding of the underlying principles before he studies the technical details in specialist works.

As the book sets out to discuss towns in developing countries it is, at the present time, necessarily concerned largely with towns in which communal organisation is inadequate. In particular the housing situation is usually bad and deteriorating, and the public services largely deficient. The question therefore arises of how far the book should take account of these urgent local problems. On reflection it has been decided not to lay great stress on them precisely because the objective is to illuminate the basic requirements rather than the present disorder. Even where the immediate situation involves a great deal of squalor, misery and illhealth, cool detached thinking is an essential element in any solution. Effective remedy of the housing situation may involve dedicated drive and sacrifice. People need to become more angry and impatient with present housing conditions than, in most countries, they yet are. Nevertheless, anger and impatience must be combined with clear thinking if they are to be fruitful.

CONTENTS

I

INTRODUCTION: TOWN PLANNING AND REGIONAL PLANNING

Various Meanings of "Planning"

As mankind starts new forms of activity it is not always easy to develop language that will suit the new needs. In consequence familiar words come to be used in new senses and are often current with more than one meaning. Because town planning and certain related activities have recently developed very rapidly, they suffer a good deal from this kind of confusion and unless the student is on his guard he can easily be misled.

The word "planning" itself, for example, has come to be used in several new senses. To many people the word "plan" probably still suggests first of all an architect's or an engineer's plan or drawing, that is to say, a precise design worked out in detail and intended to be realised exactly as designed. If it is an architect's plan it is essentially a design of something static, and though an engineer's drawing may be a design for something that moves, it will be expected that the machine, once constructed, will maintain its original character unchanged. In common speech, however, we often use "planning" in another sense. When we talk of "planning a holiday" we do not expect to decide every detail of the holiday before it starts, and we shall not be surprised if a certain amount of change takes place in the plan in the course of the holiday. In fact, the attraction of our plan may be that it combines a number of definite decisions with a certain amount of freedom of action within the general scheme.

Recent uses of the word "planning" are far more of this latter character. They presuppose a definite course of action, which brings advantages by making certain systematic decisions and presupposes that successive actions will be systematically linked. Nevertheless, this main course of action assumes that subsidiary choices will be left open and even that some of the original decisions may be modified if they prove less advantageous than was at first expected. The fundamental idea is that of carefully considered, consistent and purposeful action in the pursuit of selected objectives. Yet even among these new meanings there is considerable variation; to avoid confusion it will be worthwhile looking briefly at two or three of them.

National Planning

"National planning" is a fairly vague concept which has grown up in the last 40 years. Its essence is a movement by a government to organise development of its territory more systematically than hitherto and to take a rather longer, more penetrating, view of the country's problems and how to deal with them. Discussion about national planning, however, normally comes to consist largely of discussing which are the most important national goals and how they can best be pursued. This concern with particular goals easily obscures the fundamental nature of the process as briefly stated above.

A national plan has in some respects the maximum freedom to choose its goals and the priorities which it gives to them. It cannot have complete freedom, because the plans must start from an assessment of the country's situation, with its various assets and liabilities. But because the plan is being made by the national government it is not constrained by the actions of higher authorities within the same country.

National plans are always largely economic, because an improved economic situation is a prerequisite of the improvement of social organisation which is their other main objective. Quite a number of national plans exist, and they vary a good deal in their form, their comprehensiveness and the amount of detail into which they enter. They all, by their nature, deal with the national territory as a whole and none go very far into detail. Maps usually play a very small part in them and their main features might be said to be discussion of how to generate and direct activities.

Regional Planning

"Regional plans" consider the problems of parts of a national territory in rather the same way as national plans do, but they naturally have less freedom because they must be affected by the aims and nature of national policies. A regional plan may, it is true, seek to influence national policy (and the national plan) by demonstrating potentialities and interests within the region which the regional planners feel that the national government is not taking sufficiently into account. Nevertheless, there must always be a certain subordination of the regional plan to the national plan or policies.

"Regions" vary a good deal in area, according to what is locally considered a convenient unit for study, but normally they include a considerable stretch of territory, the geography of which is pretty varied and within which lie many communities of different kinds, including a number of towns of varying sizes. The objects of a regional plan are very much the same as those of a national plan but, because the area to be studied is smaller, they usually enter into more detail, particularly physical detail. Nevertheless, a regional plan is usually concerned mainly with activities and organisations and only in a secondary way with physical installations. On the other hand, regional plans vary a good deal and the concept of the regional plan is rapidly evolving.

Town Planning

A "town plan" deals with a more restricted area, namely, that which is of direct concern to the welfare and growth of a particular town. Nevertheless, it is like a national or regional plan in being a programme of carefully thought out and coordinated action. This may seem a surprising comment to some readers, because a "town plan" is often thought of as being primarily and almost exclusively a map. As we shall see later, however, the map of a town plan[1] is only an instrument in the whole process of town planning, which might be better described as "town management".

Continuity of Town Planning

The point made here, that town planning should be a continuous process and not an isolated operation, has not always been recognised. Until the last 30 years, in fact, town planning was usually an intermittent process, applied only to parts of the town. As a result, many communal activities, such as the laying-out of new streets or the provision of water supply, were often carried out without proper coordination and without proper consideration of future needs. In fact, town management existed, but was not systematically planned. Now it is being recognised increasingly that national planning, regional planning and town planning all reflect recognition of the need for more systematic thought on the way society is managed. In all three spheres excessive claims have sometimes been put forward and mistakes have been made, but these errors do not invalidate the attempt to apply more forethought and system. They only show that it is a difficult process that must be learnt.

These constant references to "management" may make some readers

1 It is recognised that the use of the words "town plan" in this book is not wholly satisfactory. The whole body of plans, written exposition and statement of policy which the book later advocates really requires a new expression but it has not been possible to devise a satisfactory one. This is part of the problem of the meaning of words referred to at the beginning of the chapter. The phrase "town planning" does not cause as much difficulty, but is not suitable in every context.

feel that they imply a highly paternalistic form of government, in which the lives of the town's inhabitants are managed in detail by a bureaucracy. This would be a mistaken view. The need for "management" springs from the nature of the needs of an urban community. As we shall see again and again in the course of the book, some activities can *only* be organised by the community as a whole, while in other cases rules made by the community are necessary if individual inhabitants of the town are to avoid being a nuisance to each other.

Despite an important resemblance to national and regional plans, however, town plans are very different from them in other respects. Just as regional plans are inevitably influenced by national policies, so, but in greater degree, an individual town plan must be influenced by factors in the life of the nation or region which lie outside the town. Important sections of this book will be concerned with the fact that a town planning authority and the individual town planner who works for them are not usually in a position to determine the way in which and the speed with which a town will grow. The town planner's task is predominantly to foresee the growth and change that must be expected and to ensure that they take place with as little physical dislocation and with as much efficiency and physical amenity as practicable. Nevertheless, a town planner, like a regional planner, may make an important contribution to the "higher" forms of planning (higher, that is, in the scale of national organisation) simply because the problems and demands of town planning are rarely fully appreciated until they are systematically stated and expounded.

Later in the book it will also be shown that the life of a town is necessarily a mixture of individual activities and of communal services (such as roads) which the individual cannot provide for himself. A third element, already referred to, is that the possible conflicts and collisions between individual activities make necessary the creation and enforcement of communal rules to prevent the individual activities being harmful to each other.

A further point about town plans is that they deal with the *densest* of human activities and this, as will be seen later, is one of the reasons why town plans have to deal with far more physical detail than either national plans or regional plans. In many parts of a town it is virtually impossible for any activity or building to be extended without physically disturbing something else. Any change, therefore, involves considering detail.

What is Town Planning?

In view of the confusion that exists over the nature of town planning, it may be well, even at the cost of some repetition, to start with a definition of "town planning" as it will be discussed in this book. This will provide the necessary background for a closer examination of the various aspects of preparing and implementing a town plan – two activities that should never be divorced.

(i) Town planning, then, consists in devising and subsequently carrying out a scheme of management of the town's growth and change in all the various respects in which they require either communal actions (that is to say, actions on behalf of all members of the community) or communal regulation (that is to say, the enforcement of rules to prevent people injuring each other.)

(ii) For convenience a town plan refers to a single town, but for sound practical results this must be the "actual" town, the whole of the built area, and not merely the area of the town within municipal limits that may no longer correspond with the "actual" town.

(iii) Moreover, the town plan always needs to include as much area beyond the physical town of today as will be necessary for future development. In practice this may lead to preparing a single plan for an area which includes more than one town, because they will merge in the future though they have not done so yet.

(iv) Beyond this area required for the physical siting of future growth, an analogous control must exist in neighbouring areas, or the pressure of control inside the town will lead to disorderly growth outside it.

What are the aims of a town plan? For clarity, these are best considered in two parts:

(a) The purely utilitarian requirements, such as the provision of essential communal services like roads and drainage and also the detailed regulation of buildings necessary to prevent people being a nuisance to each other. These utilitarian requirements are the essential basis for anything that is done under (b) below.

(b) What might be called the "supra-utilitarian" aspect, that is to say, all those things which contribute to making town life more than merely healthy and convenient, which help it to be pleasant and people to be happy. This aspect includes all the aesthetic sides of town planning, which are sometimes called civic design.

The various activities that come under these two heads will be discussed more fully in subsequent chapters. At this stage, however, it will be useful to emphasise one point. It is natural to feel that what is here called the "supra-utilitarian" aspect is the part that really matters and that the main failures of town planning have been on this side. No town, however, can be successful in this "supra-utilitarian" sphere unless it is efficient in the utilitarian sphere. This book will constantly emphasise practical points, not because these are the whole of the process, but because they are an essential foundation. It is only when a planner has mastered the practical side of his art that he can develop it further and make a success of the social and aesthetic aspects. Much less will be said in this book about the "supra-utilitarian" aspect, because this is bound to be much more a question of personal skill and genius, but that does not mean that its importance is underrated.

Vital Elements in Town Planning

It is worth noting that town planning as defined above includes the following elements:

(i) study of the present situation and of what may be expected in the future;

(ii) selection of a particular course of action as being the most advantageous;

(iii) consistent action over a period in accordance with the conclusions formed from (i) and (ii) above (this is sometimes called "implementation");

(iv) limitation of the action primarily to the communal field, with the consequence that there must be perpetual inter-action with the "individuals" who are active in the town. (See below Chapter VIII).

For the above purposes it is usual to prepare plans, and there is a widespread belief that these plans are the essence of the operation, but that is a misunderstanding. The plans are only one means of working out the right management policy, and this is clear if one reflects on the essential nature of such plans. As can be seen from examining typical specimens, they are primarily illustrations of *changes* which it is hoped to bring about. Normally the plans show many things besides the proposed changes, but these are shown only in order to bring out the significance of the changes and to make clear where changes are not proposed. The fact that the plans are concerned with changes implies the intention to implement them. The finding and organisation of means of implementation is an essential part of the process, which must be borne in mind at every stage.

There are two kinds of broad change with which a town planner is concerned. One is the expected physical extension of the town. For this reason, as already noted, a town plan normally covers a wider area than the physical extent of the town when the planning work begins.

Changes of Land Use in a Town

The other kind of change consists of changes of land use inside the town, such as conversion of houses into shops, replacement of shops by offices, building factories instead of other buildings or conversely. Open spaces may be built over or, more rarely, buildings may be cleared to make open spaces. All the time, varying areas will be used for transport routes, the intensity of the use varying. Some changes of land use do not affect the activities on adjoining land, but in towns, where activity is very intensive, other activities often are affected and it is for this reason that the communal authority is called in as manager and regulator. In order to understand the work of a town planning authority it is necessary to realise that, although in one respect it is concerned with every aspect of the town, it is primarily concerned with communal matters, with the ways in which cooperation is necessary or regulation of individuals is needed for the benefit of the whole. Initiative by the town planning authority is often important, but the main driving forces in the town are the activities of the "individuals" just referred to.

It has already been made clear that the plans are only a means of illustrating what the most important changes are and for that purpose are not complete in themselves. They always require verbal explanation to make clear why particular changes have been selected where alternatives were available, how far one change is dependent upon another, and so forth. Moreover, if the whole town plan does not remain a dead letter, as sometimes happens, it will gradually be carried out and the basic plans should be gradually altered to show which changes suggested on them have become reality.

Nature of the Management Required

Most important, but very difficult to present in a form which gives a vivid picture of the process as a whole, is the day-to-day management which gradually makes use of the thinking and coordinated decisions that went to the devising of the policy illustrated in the plan. No-one can be a good town planner unless he can constantly bear in mind these various aspects: first, the study and coordinated thinking; secondly, the achievement of reasoned, closely-knit decisions about the future; thirdly, the gradual working out, flexible in detail but constantly firm on the essential principles.

The whole process, of course, varies with the size of the town. Small towns often, but not always, present simple problems. On the other hand, the development of such towns is often quite slow and this makes it all the more difficult to preserve consistency of policy from year to year. Moreover, in small towns it is sometimes very difficult to raise the capital for communal services.

Broadly speaking, the bigger the town the more complex the problems, and the complexity is apt to make one think that the same basic principles do not apply. This is a great mistake; it is precisely in the big towns that the town planner needs to keep a very tight hold on his fundamental principles to prevent himself being confused by the complex details.

Is Town Planning a Modern Development?

It has already been said that town planning as defined above is a modern development. It is modern largely in the attempt to systematise, to look well ahead over the whole field and to take into account the complex modern services. There has always been some regulation of towns, but in the past it has tended to consist largely of general rules (prohibition of encroachment on the public streets, for example) combined with impressive improvements affecting limited areas only, such as the new streets cut by Haussmann in 19th century Paris, the baroque piazzas in Rome or the building of Regent Street in London. Much regulation of towns still has this limited sporadic character.

In the past there has been real private town planning, notably on the big leasehold estates of some English towns, but such private activity has always been partial and has sometimes had unfortunate effects outside its restricted sphere, for example, by forcing development unwelcome to the estate owner on to nearby unregulated land. Town planning in its modern sense must involve management by a public authority.

Is Town Planning Expensive?

From one point of view, town planning is a costly process. It clearly involves the spending of money on public services concerned with the improvement and expansion of the town. This expenditure, however, is not *caused* by town planning. It would be necessary in any event. Town planning aims at organising the expenditure and working out the most economical programme that can be devised. There are therefore reasons for regarding town planning as essential for economical public administration.

On the other hand, because town planning aims at looking ahead, it tries to face the awkward financial problems in good time. This makes people more conscious of them and can actually give the impression that the act of planning has created the problems. In truth, the pressure for town planning today derives partly from the fact that often the financial problems of town development have not been faced at the right moment, so that large parts of many modern towns have degenerated into chaos and squalor, for which people are now demanding a remedy. Because town planning tries to avoid this state of affairs and to ensure the provision of communal services in good time, it often represents an attempt to increase immediate public expenditure. But this expenditure has never been avoidable. One of the great problems of modern society is to face the need for this expenditure and to provide means for meeting it.

THE AIM OF THIS BOOK

It will be realised that town planning is a complex subject, requiring extensive knowledge of how towns work and the ability to think about them in ways to which the ordinary man is unaccustomed. This leads deeply into various complex technical matters, such as statistical forecasting, the technical evolution of industry, communal provision for social needs, the engineering aspects of drainage and road construction and so forth. It may therefore appear that town planning is exclusively a task for specialists, but there are several reasons why this is not so.

In the first place, the whole object is to produce an environment which will make possible a happy life for ordinary people. It is therefore important that all the specialist work should be constantly tested by seeing how it contributes to this simple fundamental aim, which is, however, so difficult to achieve. It is most important that each specialist should understand the problem as a whole or he will easily fail to explain the practical significance of his conclusions.

Secondly, the town planners are dependent upon the community for which they are working and the people of the community must therefore understand what the planners are doing. This is true in the narrower sense that there must be some public authority which supplies the planners with the resources for their work and possesses the powers to take the necessary measures for the management of the town. It is true also in a wider sense because the change and growth of the town depend upon the action of many individuals and organisations, whose needs and motives must be taken into account.

Even if the issues are complex, therefore, town planning problems need to be expressed in straightforward human terms. It is not, however, easy to see the general picture apart from the technical complexity of the individual issues involved. The aim of this book is to provide the general picture and, to that end, it enters as little as possible into technicalities. Its aim is rather to show where the various techniques fit in, so that each can be appropriately used.

The book is intended for readers of two kinds:

first, the general reader who wishes to understand the general issues without getting involved in technicalities;

second, the town planning student at the beginning of his course, who wishes to get a general idea of his field. It is hoped that the book will be particularly useful to young men in developing countries who find that many existing books are written largely in terms of the problem as it appears in one particular country with which the author is familiar.

Chapters II to V explain why towns are so important today, and the significance of a few broad aspects.

Chapter VI deals at length with the important question of how a town planner studies his problem.

Chapter VII sets out the essential basic legal requirements.

Chapters VIII to X explain the main factors causing change in towns and the broad implications of the changes.

Chapters XI to XIII explain the nature of certain technical problems. No attempt is made to expound specialist techniques. The aim is to make clear where each technique is applicable and roughly what it can do.

Chapters XIV to XVI explain how a policy for town management (or "town planning scheme") is worked out and how it should be used.

II

THE PRESENT-DAY IMPORTANCE OF TOWNS

The planning of towns is becoming of greater importance than ever before because of the rapid growth of towns. Urban population is expanding at a faster rate than the rate of growth of the total population and this trend can be expected to continue and indeed, in many countries, to accelerate. It will therefore be worthwhile to consider the basic reasons for this imbalance in growth. It is impossible to deal with the particular circumstances of every country, but certain influences are widely operative, and it is particularly important to understand these if the trend to urbanisation is to be grasped.

Why Economic Progress leads to Urbanisation

The fundamental factor responsible for the present increase in the population of towns is that most countries are progressing economically, even if the progress is much less rapid than is desirable and not fast enough to solve local social problems. Economic progress beyond the lowest levels means that a smaller proportion of the population is occupied in producing food and agricultural raw materials, so that more people are becoming available for other kinds of production, most of which are, and must be, carried on in towns. A natural consequence is that, even though in most countries the rural population is increasing, it tends to form, gradually, a smaller proportion of the whole. This tendency for the rural population to fall relatively has sometimes caused concern among those responsible for a country's development, but reflection will make clear that economic progress must depend upon having a smaller percentage of the people tied to food production. The occurrence of surplus population in the rural areas is not a guarantee of progress, for there may be failure to absorb them in other pursuits, but it is a condition of progress all the same.

In extreme cases, such as Afghanistan, the agricultural population probably forms, at the time of writing, more than 90% of the total. In many countries, despite the uncertainties of statistics, it evidently forms

70% or more. It may be as low as 10% in the wealthy and highly developed countries. Accordingly, it will be clear that if the agricultural population in many developing countries were to fall to even 40% of the whole, a very large number of people would be released for urban employment. This would have a startling effect on the urban population. The scale of the possible change can be illustrated by one or two examples:

In Afghanistan, with a total estimated population of about 15,000,000 (there has been no national census), the urban population is not more than a million, so that if the total remained steady and the urban population multiplied by three, it would still form only 20% of the whole. It is likely, however, that the total population is increasing every year by at least 1.5% or approximately 225,000 people. In ten years, therefore, if the urban population were to be multiplied by three, it would form only about 17% of the enlarged population.

The total population of Turkey of about 31,000,000 is increasing at approximately 2.6% per annum, or nearly 800,000 people. If, therefore, this number of people were added to the Turkish towns every year, the rural population would not be reduced in actual numbers, although it would become a diminishing proportion of the whole.

Agricultural Progress and Town Growth

The position must not be over-simplified. Certain contrary trends do exist. In some countries, particularly in Africa, there are still considerable reserves of agricultural land, so that, as the agricultural population expands, it can also expand its agricultural means of subsistence. Nevertheless, even in such countries, the urban population tends to become an increasing proportion of the whole. This is because efforts are constantly being made to raise the incomes of the agricultural population and, to the extent that these efforts are successful, they inevitably raise the demand of the farmers for non-agricultural products, mainly from the towns. A modest rise in income may have striking effects because it tends to bring the farmer above the bare subsistence level. An increase of only 5% in his income may have the effect of doubling the proportion of his income that he spends in the town. In a country with very little industry most of the trade of the towns depends upon the purchasing power of the farmers, so that a change of this kind might increase the trade of a town by as much as 25% even if the total number of the town's rural customers did not change.

The efforts that are being made to improve agricultural methods very often have the effect of increasing the demand for town products for purely agricultural purposes. Artificial fertilizers are often manufactured in towns and more complex agricultural implements generally mean greater reliance upon town sources of supply as opposed to past periods when implements could more easily be made in the village. It is impossible to quote general figures about movements of this kind without their being misleading, as conditions vary very much from area to area and can change quickly in any one district; but such trends are factors which the town planner needs to understand if he is to make intelligent forecasts for the future.

Many efforts to raise agricultural incomes naturally take the form of increasing agricultural productivity per head, so that the individual can get a better reward for his labour. This may mean simply that the same number of men get a larger return from the same area of land, but in fact it very often means that a better return can be secured from the same area *with fewer men.* Increase of agricultural production may therefore be accompanied by a fall in the number employed over a wide area and, even if the agricultural area expands, the number of agricultural workers may not increase at all, or not proportionately to the expansion of the area.

It is true that in certain circumstances intensification of cultivation may increase the number of workers per hectare. The most common case of this is perhaps certain districts near large towns which take to the intensive cultivation of vegetables. On the whole, however, this is a minor influence. In fact, although intensive cultivation of things like vegetables is common near big towns, the attractiveness of these towns, by drawing off many former agriculturalists, may speed up agricultural mechanisation and so reduce agricultural employment with exceptional speed.

Agricultural Underemployment

It also needs to be recognised that many agricultural communities already contain more people than they really need for the efficient cultivation of the land. This readily happens if improved health services cause a better rate of survival while, at the same time, the means of production are inelastic and alternative sources of employment are not readily available. Moreover, many communities use the whole of their labour force at only a few peak seasons such as seedtime and harvest. A single change, such as the introduction of mechanical reaping of wheat, may mean that an appreciable number of workers become wholly redundant instead of being needed seasonally. They may not quit the agricultural community at once, but such groups constitute reserves of potential emigrants which can cause startling waves of urban migration when the prospects in the cities appear to be particularly good or those in the rural areas become particularly bad.

Population Increase

Finally, one must take account of the all but universal tendency for population generally to increase. From this point of view, there is no such thing as a stable community and the excess of births over deaths has no necessary relation to the existence of local economic opportunities. On the contrary, the improvement of health services means that many agricultural communities are tending to increase their numbers by, say, 25% every ten years despite the fact that the local means of production may be inelastic or even declining. Even where the local means of rural production can still be expanded it is usually difficult to provide for expansion of employment at the same rate as the growth of the local population.

The same excess of births over deaths exists in cities where, in fact, it is often higher than in the countryside because health conditions are better, though this difference is not necessarily permanent. It is startling to realise how much most cities must be expected to grow even if there is no migration. Many a city will increase 25% in ten years without migration, with the consequent expectation that, from the same cause, it will increase by a further 20% at least in the ten years following that.

Normally, of course, a growing city attracts immigration. Natural increase plus immigration may well cause a city to increase by 50% in ten years, while 100% increase in the same time is not uncommon where growth influences are strong.

It may be argued that the growing influence of birth control will gradually modify the natural growth of the population. It will be of particular interest in the next ten years to see how powerful its influence can become. At present, however, there is no evidence that birth control can be expected to have radical effects quickly, and it needs to be borne in mind that in many developing countries in the immediate future the death rate may fall more rapidly than the birth rate, so that the present rate of natural increase will rise. In any event, it will be appreciated that changes in the proportions of rural and urban employment would continue to encourage the growth of towns, even if the growth of the population as a whole sank to nil.

"Pull" and "Push" in Migration to Towns

There has been a good deal of argument about how far the increase of urban population has been due to the "pull" of employment opportunities, facilities for education and amenities in the towns, and how far it has been due to the "push" of unemployment and poor conditions in the rural areas. In particular places, "pull" may be of greater importance because a particular town happens to offer exceptional opportunities. A town planner should always consider how strong the "pull" of his own town is. In general, however, it is important to recognise the importance of the "push" factor. Agricultural progress is likely to decrease agricultural employment while increasing the demand for town products in the rural areas. Inability to obtain work in the country, or to obtain it on favourable conditions, is thus an important motive for moving to a town. Poor conditions in a town may yet be better than the prospects in the countryside. In assessing the future of a town, therefore, it is important to assess the prospective changes in agricultural incomes and agricultural employment in neighbouring districts.

It can be argued, of course, that lack of agricultural employment does not necessarily imply lack of *rural* employment and that a sound social policy will seek to minimise the extent to which it does. Those who hold this view draw attention to the present importance of rural handicrafts in some areas and their potentialities as the basis of rural industries. Two arguments are generally advanced for making the most of these potentialities. On the one hand, it is certainly desirable that rural communities should not be unnecessarily impoverished through the supersession of rural crafts by urban factories. On the other hand, towns as they exist today have their own evils and it can be contended that they should be kept to a minimum. These views have a certain amount of force, but nevertheless they are unlikely to affect seriously the dominant trend to urbanisation. In the first place, for trading and industrial purposes towns have indisputable practical advantages, if only because they bring people into convenient proximity for joint activities, while their existing faults are not irremediable. In the second place, there seems to be plenty of evidence that a very large proportion of the human race is more attracted by town life than by rural life, despite all the difficulties of the former.

The above is necessarily a very brief and incomplete account of why the trend to urbanisation is so important today. The main point is that the town planner should realise how important it is and how strong the growth factors are. If one understands the basic trend, it will be evident why town planning should be a constantly growing preoccupation at the present time.

III

THE TOWN IN RELATION TO ITS REGION

Areas of Influence of Towns

A town is always a centre of activity for a considerable area and, in many cases, its sphere of influence varies for different purposes. There is usually an area close to the town from which people come for all kinds of trading. In addition, the town may send certain types of manufactured goods for much greater distances, both within the country and for export. In a large area smaller towns may serve the simpler trading needs, while people resort to the bigger towns for more specialised goods and wholesale trading. A common exercise is to draw maps of the spheres of influence of towns. This is a valuable technique, which illustrates in a useful way the relative roles of different towns, but it should not be used by itself, since it can lead to dangerous oversimplification and also suggests a misleading degree of stability. One cannot really understand a town's influence unless one understands how far its trading extends for different purposes. Local and distant trading may have quite different shares of total trade in neighbouring towns and it is easy to obscure such points.

Changes in Areas of Influence

One danger is that the preparation of such maps may serve to mislead their users because they necessarily show the picture at a particular moment without regard to current changes. The areas of influence depicted on the map may be expanding or contracting rapidly, and these dynamic properties will not appear on the map, which is necessarily presented some time after the relevant statistics have been gathered. This is another case which calls for a warning and a lucid explanation to accompany the map. It cannot be stressed too often that the conditions influencing the preparation of a plan are changing while the plan is being drawn; sometimes these changes are influenced by the planning investigations since the latter draw attention to what is happening and cause people to change their views in consequence.

An interesting comparison is afforded by two towns in south Turkey.

Adana, with a population rather over 300,000, is a big regional centre supplying all sorts of specialised services to a wide surrounding area, even within the spheres of influence of smaller towns which supply less specialised services to their neighbourhoods. About 80 kilometres away, Mersin, with approximately 90,000 people, is much less important as a regional centre of Adana's type. Nevertheless, because it is an important port, it has commercial relations of another kind with an area at least as large as that which Adana serves. Because there is a refinery at Mersin, its influence in the petroleum trade extends further still.

It is also important that a town's sphere of influence may be changing in opposite senses in different trades. For example, if the agricultural area is prosperous, local trade may be increasing. At the same time, long distance trade in manufactured goods may be diminishing as a result of the emergence of new centres of production. There may be migratory movements as a result of these changes or there may be changes in the skills required from people remaining in the town. The balance of change may be favourable or unfavourable, but in either case it is important to know what the separate trends are, so that provision can be made for the expanding ones, despite the fact that other activities may be dying.

Significance of a Town's Relation to its Region

The relation of a town to the region in which it stands is important to the town planner, who cannot comprehend the life and trends of the town unless he acquires an understanding of its external relationships. These affiliations form an essential element in any attempt to judge what is going to happen to the town. Their study also provides a valuable test of proposals for development, for it can help in maintaining a realistic view of what can and cannot be done.

An understanding of the various bases of a town's trade and industry can be very important in working out a good plan. This is particularly true if a town is changing rapidly, so that activities which used to be fairly distinct are beginning to become less well-defined and somewhat jumbled. If the town has an important retail trade with a neighbouring area, the needs of that trade must be specially considered, particularly as regards such a matter as ease of access by people visiting the town. Other trades, growing and commanding considerable capital resources, may tend to invade and congest the retail area, despite the fact that provision could better be made for their needs in other ways. This care for a particular kind of trade may be all the more important when, although stable and prosperous in itself, it is tending to become a smaller element in the life of a growing town and may be unnecessarily disturbed by the rapidly growing components of the commercial community.

Quite apart from the planning aspect, the governing body of a well-managed town will be conscious of the diversity of groups which its community serves and will be anxious to retain the town's reputation for good service. In order to carry conviction, it is essential that these good intentions be translated into convenient physical arrangements. This means that the town planner should be alive to the issues and must have convinced his municipality of the importance of the physical adjustments involved.

Competition between Communities

In every country, the various communities are constantly changing their relations with each other. To some extent, the local communities are helping one another and often to a great extent taking part in a struggle for survival. Every town is, to a degree, a factor in this interplay of forces and is always subject to the influence of the national government's attempts to manage the development of the country's social and economic life.

Relations with the National Government

The influence of the national government on the town will be less intelligent than it might be unless the government is informed about the town's life, evolution and potentialities. It is important, therefore, that each municipality should keep the government informed fully on these matters. The town planner must naturally take an important part in the presentation if the facts are to be properly evaluated. This is not to suggest that the national government will necessarily do what the town wishes, however well the case is presented, but it is certainly more likely to do so if the local situation and its potentialities are fully understood. Moreover, if the desires of the municipal government cannot be met, the town fathers will certainly be able to adjust their policies better if they understand the point of view of the national government and the difficulties it sees.

One very likely occurrence, at the present time, is that the national government will have to press certain developments on the town. This may even involve the transfer of population from an overcrowded area, thus introducing into the town's life an element which the town authorities could not have foreseen.

To be useful, however, exchanges between a town and the national government must consist in realistic debate. If the town confines itself to uncritically blowing its own trumpet, the simple result will be that it ceases to be listened to and that its comments will be deliberately discarded as unreliable. This will do its interests more harm than good.

All this may appear to involve excessive demands on human nature. It may be argued that discussion of this quality rarely takes place, and that it is too much to expect anything of the kind as a general standard. This is painfully true, but debate of this kind is urgently required and, in its absence, national governments will continue to make decisions affecting the lives of urban communities, possibly on an unsound basis. The growing importance of urbanisation has been stressed and this is bound to cause fresh needs, one of which is that there should be much fuller and more informed discussion of urban affairs. In this whole sphere of urbanisation, we must guard against being too much influenced by the standards of the past. If intelligent debate is urgently needed, the first thing to do is to recognise this and thus to create an essential condition for getting it going.

Influence of National Population Growth

Reference has been made above to the influence of the national population problem on the town. This is a matter which is likely to prove of increasing importance in the next 20 years, as increasing populations cause greater and greater problems, particularly because the overspill from the agricultural community will often increase rapidly. From the town planner's point of view, this raises a number of points of interest. In order to judge the future of local trade, it is necessary to be aware of the probable changes in the local population. It may increase or it may diminish, and a present increase may change shortly into a fall. A fall in the local population does not mean that there will necessarily be a fall in trade with it. Increasing agricultural incomes may offset the effects of the fall, but clearly the needs of a small well-to-do population and of a big population with much lower standards of living will not be the same. To understand the way the town's trade is going to develop, one must follow such changes carefully.

The most important influence on population is likely, however, to be the increasing overspill of rural population which must find its future employment in the towns. (The reasons for this trend are discussed on pp. 19-21.) The town may find itself obliged to absorb migrants either from its own sphere of influence or from more distant areas, or both, and it should be noted that the movement is as likely to be a result of "push" from the rural areas as of "pull" from the towns. In other words, the towns must do their best to absorb migrants, whether they are anxious to do so or not; if necessary, the development of employment in the town will have to be pushed ahead faster than it would otherwise have gone. This is primarily a matter for the national government, as part of the process of making adjustments between different areas, but any such movement is bound to have important effects in the town planning sphere. It will mean that the network of services will have to be extended more rapidly than would otherwise have been the case. Moreover, rural migrants arriving in these conditions are likely to be poor but yet to need houses quickly. This will have an important effect on the kind and number of houses needed, and also on the means required for providing them. It is likely to involve more provision of houses by public authorities, because even cooperatives will be unable to do what is necessary fast enough.

Certain physical characteristics may be foreseen which will, eventually, absolutely limit the population that can be accommodated in a town. The sooner such factors are recognised the more successfully the consequences may be met and dealt with. Such limitations may be imposed by the amount of water available in an area or actual restrictions of area which would eventually involve a density of population which could no longer be considered safe or efficient. When an absolute ceiling of this kind can be anticipated, the national government may have to be called upon, by the town's authorities, to provide a solution to the problem of controlling the growth of population.

The Difficulty of Controlling Migration

Usually, the most obvious source of this population growth is the migration from rural areas or less prosperous urban areas. To governments whose organisation is as yet not geared to the demands of a complex industrial society, the obvious action may appear to be to control migration by law, but there are serious difficulties and dangers in this method. Laws of this kind attempted in the past have been largely unsuccessful because of economic pressures of the labour-starved industries and the unemployed migrants. The industries will use every possible subterfuge to obtain workers. Those displaced from the farms because of mechanisation, or just plain surplus of labour, will cause serious problems and will certainly dislocate the economy by forcing the government to care for them. In practice, the only successful method of reducing immigration to any one town is to make other towns more attractive and profitable for the potential urban dweller. Availability of employment, housing, and convenient transportation all contribute to the enticement of people to an area.

An illustration of a solution to the problem of migration guidance is now being developed in Iran. Teheran, the capital, almost tripled its population in twenty years. The growth has been so rapid that the municipal government has been unable to supply basic public services. Only recently, the High Planning Council of the Iranian Government has concluded that the maximum water supply available will be able to accommodate no more than 5,000,000 people, or about twice the population in 1966. The limitation of the size of the city has, by necessity, become a problem of the national government.

One action taken by the government was to plan the construction of an iron-smelting plant close to Isfahan, the fabled centre of ancient Persia. Isfahan now has a population of something over 450,000 and can eventually handle about three times as many people. Other efforts are being made to increase arable agricultural land and decentralise government operations in order to disseminate the people now employed in the capital.

Influence of a Town on its Surroundings

In this chapter the town has been considered primarily as a centre for an area around it. It needs to be borne in mind, however, that a town, besides serving its area, also influences it. This is particularly noticeable where a town is large or where its primary function is not acting as a district centre, but some other purpose such as the development of a local mineral industry. Reference has already been made to the fact that a town may influence local agriculture by stimulating the cultivation of vegetables or by competing with agriculture for the local labour supply. It may also cause changes in the rural area by works designed for urban purposes, such as the impounding of a river to provide an urban water supply.

The influence of the town on its neighbourhood is likely to be particularly important when the town changes its role. For some time a town may remain a small community, providing local services but expanding little and consuming little of the local produce. If it then develops a big industrial population it will become an important market in itself, whereas formerly the local farmers had to send their produce much further afield. It may also be able to provide new kinds of services in such spheres as banking and education, which formerly had to be sought at a distance.

IV

NOTES ON METROPOLITAN AREAS AND DECENTRALISATION

Rapid Growth of Very Large Towns

One of the most important and most obvious tendencies of the present day is the rapid growth of very large towns, by which phrase is meant, for the purposes of the present chapter, towns which each have a population of a million or more, and particularly the "conurbations", where a series of amorphous settlements grow together into a sort of ill-organised urban rash. This is evidently a very powerful tendency and therefore deeply rooted in our present evolution. Moreover, it is remarkably widespread. Turkey, until recently a country with little urban life outside Istanbul, is likely by the end of the present century to have five towns of a million or more, Istanbul by itself having perhaps three million people by then. Afghanistan, which for centuries has had no large towns, is likely to have a million people in its capital at the same date. Egypt, still a comparatively poor country, has four million people in Cairo, and India, despite its tremendous poverty, has quite a list of towns over the million mark, including one of the biggest conurbations in the world.

Why this Growth is Controversial

In many countries, both official and unofficial opinion is uncertain as to how far this tendency should be welcomed. A substantial body of opinion is vaguely in favour of limiting the big towns or even of decentralising them. This body of opinion has so far had a negligible effect on the trends, but it is evidently of great importance to be clear whether this fundamentally critical view is soundly based or not. The whole subject is full of difficulties, but certain basic realities can be perceived and every town planner should be familiar with them.

The main reasons why many people dislike very big towns are as follows.

(a) In certain respects very big towns are more difficult to organise than smaller ones; because they have recently attracted so much migration their organisation is in many cases in some confusion, presenting a most daunting picture of what urban problems can amount to. There is an instinctive, though not very rational, feeling that the problems of small towns are easier to deal with and that life in them is healthier in the broad sense of that word.

(b) In addition there is a fear that a country's whole development will be dominated by the growth of one big town, to the detriment of smaller but deserving communities. This fear sometimes has a rational foundation and sometimes it does not. That is to say that in some countries the concentration of much of the development in one urban centre may have caused the development of the country's economy as a whole to be less than the optimum. Elsewhere, it is at least doubtful whether this is true, and the hostility simply reflects the natural jealousy of other communities which are doing less well, apparently through no fault of their own.

(c) There is a fear that the magnet effect of the big town helps to increase rural migration and that the latter causes depopulation and decay of the rural areas. This is in most cases a mistaken view based on the belief that, because migration from the rural areas is so large, it must result in a fall of the rural population, but this is rarely so. More often than not, rural populations are still rising and even where they are falling this is not necessarily a disaster. The fall may simply reflect a necessary rationalisation of the agricultural labour force, with increased prosperity for those who remain on the land. It will have been noted from Chapter II, "The Present-Day Importance of Towns", that the attractions of city life are not necessarily (in fact, perhaps, not usually) the most important stimulus to migration from rural areas.

(d) In addition, there is jealousy of the big towns simply because of their success in attracting people. Even when an immigrant is not doing very well in a big town he rarely feels that he will better his lot by moving to a smaller town or back to the countryside. He still feels the big town is the best option.

Advantages of very large Towns

These fears and criticisms should not be allowed to hide the fact that very big towns, despite all their defects and difficulties, have most important advantages. In the first place a large urban community undoubtedly facilitates certain types of economic organisation, especially the starting of specialised trades serving only a small proportion of the community, so that only in a large settlement have they a reasonable number of customers conveniently close at hand. This is particularly important in the development of a country like Kenya or Afghanistan, which for long did not have any large urban community at all.

It is also much easier to organise higher education in a large community. For this reason it is often the only practicable solution to site a country's first university in the largest town.

Then in the early stages of developing public services, particularly roads, air services and electric power, it is inevitable that these should be concentrated first of all in the largest town, where the speediest economic return can be secured. This is not merely a question of securing enough revenue to service the necessary loan, it is also a question of using the new service to give the quickest possible economic stimulus. In all developing countries speed of development must be a major consideration.

Granted, then, that very large towns have real advantages, is the reaction against them simply misconceived, or is there a real basis for criticism?

Disadvantages of Very Large Towns

The best way of achieving an objective view is perhaps to look at the matter for a moment from the general national planning point of view, rather than from that of big towns in particular. One of the reasons for developing national planning, and then for developing regional planning as a corollary, is that the welfare of various parts of a country tends to be unequal. This, besides causing hardship to local populations, may also lead to the neglect of valuable forms of local development simply because there is no local agency capable of undertaking them. In other words, it is part of the basis of national and regional planning that the whole area of the country needs to be surveyed in order to ascertain where extra stimuli need to be applied and where salvage measures are needed. This immediately shows that the development of the big cities should not be considered in isolation, but assessed against the background of the country's development as a whole.

This chapter began with the comment that the very big towns were both a spontaneous and a very powerful development. Because the movement is so dramatic and has so much momentum it naturally tends to attract an undue proportion of investment simply because the big towns present the most obvious, if sometimes deceptive, investment opportunities. This reflects the fact that the private investor, through ignorance of the investment field as a whole, is always inclined to over-invest in whatever appears to be the best immediate prospect; but in addition, government organisations are under the same temptation to concentrate their resources in the most obvious sphere of development without a proper assessment of merits.

The converse of this tendency to over-invest in the obvious development lines is a tendency to neglect real but less obvious possibilities that are available elsewhere. There is, of course, the corresponding error of assuming that, simply because an area has been neglected, it *must* offer good investment openings. That has done its own share of damage. Nevertheless, intelligent management of a country's development always involves the judicious stimulation of areas that are lagging. Even where this is not justifiable on strictly economic grounds (because there are alternative possible uses of the resources concerned), it may be justifiable on welfare grounds.

The Question of Creating Alternative Centres of Attraction

This joins up with another consideration. If one is seriously concerned to limit the growth of very big towns and perhaps eventually to decentralise them, there is only one way of achieving this: to make other centres more attractive, so that there ceases to be a powerful motive for going to the big town and the big town only.

There is still reluctance to squarely face the fact that this is the only realistic solution and some people still talk about such measures as registering the populations of big towns and restricting entry to them. This to put it mildly, is a formidable administrative undertaking, for the reasons discussed briefly on p. 28. It has, in fact, been done in restricted areas under the exceptional conditions of war and in developed countries. In peacetime, however, it raises serious practical problems. How is illicit infiltration in a town to be prevented, and if an illicit migrant is found, what is to be done with him? To return him to his place of origin is difficult and also probably useless as he may have no means of subsistence there. In peacetime, therefore, and particularly in developing countries, formal regulation of migration must be regarded as impracticable, besides being a serious waste of scarce administrative manpower.

This is not to say that the right solution, namely, to make other centres more competitive with the very big town, is at all an easy one. On the other hand, in order to study the possibilities of this approach, it is necessary to examine the development potentials of various areas, and this needs to be done in any event. It is worthwhile to examine the main requirements for creating a competitive developing centre.

It goes without saying, of course, that the centre selected must have certain basic advantages as regards situation, communications etc. The more difficult task is to endow it with the characteristics which make it a positive influence in the working-out of new development projects.

No centre can become a serious point of growth unless it is successful in competing for the establishment of new industrial development. For this purpose it must be able to supply certain basic needs, such as the requirements of new industries for electricity, water, drainage and good communications. It is true that in case of need a new industry can find its own electricity or water, but if we are to keep our eye on the main objective, which is to make the area attractive to developers who were not previously disposed to settle in it, it becomes evident that services of this kind must be readily available.

Education is no less important. In a developing country, where the educational organisation is still far from complete, the special educational advantages of living in a big town tend to be very important, and this applies, though in somewhat different ways, to both rich and poor. In the early stages of industrialisation, moreover, technical education is of great importance and the new industrial establishments tend to be drawn to the big towns both because they offer the best technical instruction and because they already have the largest pools of scarce technicians. For a new centre to become attractive, therefore, it needs to offer very positive educational advantages, in both the general and technical fields.

The Problem of Resources for a Constructive Urban Policy

A conflict of aims now becomes apparent, which is due to the universal difficulty of finding sufficient resources for improving and developing town organisation in all the various ways that this is necessary. On the one hand, there is evidently a strong case for a special effort to reorganise the very big towns, which may be conurbations of several merged towns, in order to improve the conditions of life there. But if this is done it will easily absorb so much of the available money and skilled personnel that there will be none left for building up other centres.

At the same time, the effort required for making other centres more attractive will in a number of respects appear less clearly productive. It is of the essence of such an operation that physical resources, such as electric power, and human services, such as education, should be developed in advance of needs, as opposed to the filling of obvious gaps which must be the main aim in the very big towns. The more or less emotional desire to restrict the very big towns is rarely based on hard calculation of the advantages of doing so or of the requirements for success. Usually, therefore, the obvious and pressing needs of the very big towns win the battle and mop up the available resources.

It must be added that in many cases the available resources and organisation are so limited that they fail to meet even the needs of the very big towns. This is one of the major crises of the modern world.

The troubles of the very big towns have multiple causes, among which sheer failure to understand what is happening plays a big part. Firstly, few countries have a detailed understanding of their own economic evolution, even if they understand the main trends, so that they are not fully aware of the causes leading to the formation of very big towns. In particular, they have not expected, and do not fully understand, the forces behind the widespread migration from the rural areas. Secondly, in the consideration of national affairs, municipal organisation and finance do not usually receive much emphasis. In fact they are often felt to be an unfortunate distraction from the drive for basic economic development and are consequently neglected. Thirdly, these very big and complex towns are difficult to understand, particularly if their development has gone a long way with little control, so that there is a great deal of "disentangling" to be done. After such a period of inadequate control, moreover, phenomena such as "squatting" (see pp. 78-80 below) have probably grown up which are very difficult to deal with, even if the municipal administration is highly developed.

For all these reasons, it is difficult to achieve, in very big towns, the basis of sound continuous management outlined in Chapter I. As compared with middle-sized or small towns, their problems are so much more complex and intractable that they give the impression of being of a totally different kind. This does not appear to be true, but the complexity is so great that few of the conurbations of the world have yet been thoroughly understood and it is rare for them to have developed an adequate planning administration.

Certainly, if a student wishes to understand the problems of very big towns and conurbations, he had better begin by studying those of smaller towns. Accordingly, this book will not lay special stress on the very big town, but will mainly discuss the genus "town" in general. Perhaps the time has not yet come when the special problems of very big towns can be adequately discussed in a general way.

V

NEW TOWNS

To many people there is something splendid about the idea of creating an entirely new town, free of the disorder and dilapidation which clutter parts of every existing town. The period since 1945 has seen the deliberate creation of new towns on a scale which has probably not been equalled since the Greco-Roman period. These new towns have attracted widespread interest, more indeed than they really deserve in the light of the contribution that they can make to the town planning problem as a whole. There is consequently a danger that the establishment of new towns will be attempted as a matter of prestige in circumstances where some other form of activity would be more useful.

It is therefore important to consider in what circumstances the creation of a new town is justified.

Specialised New Towns

First, a new town is the only solution when it is necessary to start a non-agricultural activity in a large uninhabited area. There have been several recent examples in both Canada and Australia as a result of the need to start mineral workings in remote and climatically unfavourable places. These communities are generally quite small now that mineral-working is so highly mechanised, and their physically unfavourable surroundings often largely prevent the growth of an associated agricultural community. Consequently it is not easy for such places to develop a diversified social life and they rarely become flourishing sub-centres in the more general sense.

The next simplest case results from the irrigation of a large uninhabited area. This involves the immigration of cultivators who, in addition to the villages in which they live, need towns as commercial and service centres. There is comparatively little difficulty in getting such towns started, and their life tends to be fuller and more varied than that of the mining towns referred to above. However, very often they grow comparatively slowly, the more complex local services being already established in some older town at a distance, which manages to maintain its established position because it possesses the know-how and the commercial connection. Growth beyond the simplest type of sub-centre is likely to depend upon the new town becoming a communications centre for a wider area or on the development of local manufacture.

New Towns for Overspill

These straightforward utilitarian cases have little to do with the vogue of new towns today. The most interesting new town creations (still limited to a few countries) have been a reaction to the wave of urbanisation which is sweeping over so many lands. In the circumstances of the country concerned, the establishment of new towns has appeared to be a means of securing a better distribution of population. A vague belief has consequently grown that new towns are some kind of a help with town planning problems. In particular, it is believed that they can help to stem the growth of the large conurbations; where the necessary improvements to a congested conurbation would cause a large overspill of population, many feel that it would be better to settle these people in new communities rather than let them increase the conurbation's spread by settling on its edge.

Interest in new towns thus tends to be based on two rather vague ideas. The first is a dislike of the very large conurbation and the desire to find at least a partial alternative to it. The second, a not very conscious or rational reaction, is a feeling that the smaller towns of the country are not suitable as growth centres.

Few Towns wholly New

Despite this last view, it is important to notice that many so-called "new" towns have not been new in the sense that the site previously had no population except a few villagers. Some of the British "new towns" had pre-existing nuclei with as many as 20,000 inhabitants. Moreover, there is no sharp line between the wholly new town, starting from a very small or nonexistent nucleus and what the British call an "expanded town", in which a fair-sized existing town is deliberately selected for enlargement because it provides a sound base and can therefore be more easily added to.

"Forced Growth" the Basic Feature

Thus the essence of a "new town" is not whether there is a nucleus already. The main point is the decision to force the growth of the town by deliberate government action and thus to attract development that would otherwise have taken place elsewhere. This is an essential clue in understanding what justifies the creation of a new town.

There is another important clue in the nature of the government activity which must underlie a successful new town project. First of all, the government must see to it that factories and other sources of employment settle in the selected growth area instead of elsewhere. Otherwise there will be no growth over and above what would have taken place spontaneously. It is therefore useless to consider a new town programme unless the government is in a position to influence the distribution of employment in this way. Moreover, unless employment in the new centre can be built up fairly rapidly, its influence on the distribution of employment over the country as a whole will be negligible. At best it will assist the welfare of a limited district which has been in a state of depression.

This problem of creating employment in the new centre links up with two other problems which we have noted elsewhere. In Chapter IV ("Notes on Metropolitan Areas and Decentralisation") we have seen that the whole problem of the decentralisation of very large towns presents serious difficulties, some of which are beyond the powers of many developing countries with limited administrative resources. Elsewhere, we shall repeatedly have to note that one of the unsolved problems of the modern world is how to devote enough of a society's resources to the development and better organisation of towns.

New Towns must be part of a larger Programme

Thirdly, it needs to be recognised that the establishment of a new town can never replace other forms of town planning work. This can be illustrated by the new towns around London, which were designed to assist with the decentralisation of that city. In one sense these new towns were a major success, because they demonstrated that, up to a certain point, people, factories and offices could be moved out of London, a matter on which many had previously been sceptical. A real beginning was therefore made with decentralisation, but simultaneously Britain was going through a phase of rapid economic change and development, as a result of which new sources of employment sprang up in London itself, additional migrants were attracted, and in the upshot no *net* decentralisation was achieved. If anything, the effort and the interest of creating the new towns distracted attention from the study of London's problems and London's role in Great Britain, with the consequence that the major problem of reorganising London on a healthier and more efficient basis was treated only superficially during a vital period of ten years, at the end of which it had become more intractable than ever.

The moral is that the establishment of new towns can never relieve the government of the responsibility of reorganising its conurbations. New towns can only be fully successful if they are part of a much larger programme for the reorganisation and development of the nation's urban life as a whole.

The fact that the British have been so successful in establishing a proportion of their new industry in new towns and in depressed areas has led to an interesting further problem which has not yet been resolved. The more prosperous of the established conurbations, such as that around Birmingham, are themselves in need of reorganisation which must include some decentralisation. These areas have already parted with the more mobile sections of their industry to the new towns and the depressed areas, and that makes the remaining units more difficult to move.

This hammers home the fact that one cannot get far with the question of whether to establish a new town without studying the comparative roles and fortunes of all the towns in the country. This is necessary simply in order to judge how far they are likely to develop spontaneously, an essential factor in considering whether some of them should have their development forcibly promoted or whether, as an alternative, new centres should be set up in competition with them.

The word "competition" is important. A new town will only be successful if it competes effectively with existing towns and proves as attractive and efficient as they are.

Selection of Possible Nuclei for New Towns

The problems of very large towns are so serious and so perplexing that in many countries they have attracted most of the attention that the government could spare for town planning matters. The problems of the smaller towns are usually less acute and often they have fallen behind in the competition for growth. In consequence, the character and potentialities of the smaller towns have never been carefully assessed, though obviously they all ought to be considered as possible growth centres before the decision is taken to promote growth on an entirely new "green field" site. Such a study of the towns leads into the field of regional planning with which this book does not attempt to deal. Assuming, however, that the result of a regional study is a *prima facie* case for concluding that the existing distribution of town growth is unsatisfactory, several other matters need to be considered before it is possible to conclude that steps should be taken to promote the growth of some centres and to retard that of others. The main questions are as follows:

(i) Has the government the necessary ability to influence the location of new sources of employment?

(ii) Can the necessary administrative and financial resources be made available in the selected growth centre without crippling necessary town development work elsewhere?

(iii) What local organisation is necessary in order to push through the communal parts of the necessary development programme, without which the establishment of new sources of employment is bound to be a failure?

Question (i) has been touched on above and involves questions of economic management which are outside the scope of this book.

Question (ii) involves the whole question of the best use of inadequate resources of finance and skilled personnel. There are certain reasons why scarce skilled manpower and limited finance may be more advantageously used for the control and improvement of existing growth centres rather than for the development of new ones. This is a very serious dilemma and turns on whether the development of the main conurbations is broadly under control or not.

The Management Problem in Conurbations

One reason why the big conurbations presently cause so much alarm is that they are often developing much more rapidly than the machinery for managing them; they have been getting increasingly out of control and conditions in them have been worsening rapidly, particularly housing and health. It may therefore be more or less imperative that the first effort should be one to establish some control and improvement in the conurbations, and in a developing country this effort may for the immediate future absorb nearly all the available manpower and finance. Anything left over will probably be absorbed by the lesser, but still serious, problems in the smaller towns of the country.

These difficulties are not a reason for neglecting altogether the desirability of establishing new towns. Rather, they show that the strategy of a country's town planning work needs to be worked out on a broad basis. From the start much attention must be devoted to building-up the necessary organisation and skilled personnel, and the programme of executive work must be carefully planned in the light of the increasing availability of trained manpower. Simultaneously, the necessary finance and other resources must be carefully built up. In the light of these problems, the establishment of new towns is unlikely to be awarded the highest priority save in connection with specific physical developments (the new mineral workings and irrigated areas referred to at the beginning of the chapter, and sometimes the establishment of a big industrial plant remote from an existing town).

As far as point (iii) above is concerned, certain aspects of the detailed organisation of new town work will also tend to encourage caution in plunging into it.

British Expanded Towns

In the British expanded towns the amount of "forced growth" is comparatively small in relation to the size of the existing town. The aim, that is to say, is more likely to be doubling the existing town than multiplying it by four or five, not to speak of building up from a minimal nucleus of 5,000 people or less. In these circumstances the existing municipality can often be used as the main executive agency for expansion, provided that it already has a strong and well-developed organisation and can readily recruit additional qualified and experienced technical staff, so that the municipality's normal scale of operations can be much increased. In most developing countries it has not yet been possible to develop mature municipalities of this kind, and experienced personnel with the necessary qualifications cannot readily be obtained.

Special Development Corporations

Developing countries may therefore be inclined to adopt the other British method, by which the central government creates *ad hoc* corporations for the express purpose of building new towns. This certainly sidesteps the problem of rapidly strengthening an inherently weak and undeveloped municipal life, an operation which it is always difficult to carry through quickly. (In fact there is no generally valid recipe for carrying it through at all.) On the other hand, it is easy to overestimate the extent to which the difficulties can be evaded in this way. In particular, if skilled staff is scarce, the change does nothing to ease the scarcity. Moreover, the establishment of a new town corporation involves setting-up a responsible and competent management of a kind of which there is little experience. The management of the corporation must show great executive efficiency and drive, but must also be fully accountable to the national government, from which the whole of its funds are necessarily derived.

Finance

The nature of the financial operations involved needs to be thoroughly appreciated before the project is decided upon. It will be evident from what has been said above that a new town is useless unless it grows fairly fast, since otherwise it will not have the necessary effect of altering the country's spontaneous urban development to a significant extent. If a new town project is started at all, therefore, it must be financed sufficiently generously to enable the work to proceed rapidly, and the supply of finance must be assured over quite a period of years. Otherwise the new town management cannot ensure the necessary continuity of work. This is another reason why new town projects should be considered in the light of the town development situation as a whole and the financial demands that that will make in other areas.

The Need for Drive

Finally it needs to be stressed that, just because new town development involves pushing development in various ways in which it would not take place spontaneously, it can only succeed by overcoming a certain inertia. The less development is already taking place in the selected area, the more the operation involves overcoming obstacles which at present are hindering growth. It is not sufficient to find what appears to be a good centre for promoting speedy growth. There must be reasons why growth is not taking place faster already. These need to be realistically analysed and the new town project must include careful measures to overcome these difficulties. Otherwise, despite the most careful preparation, the project will hang fire.

The superficial attractiveness of new towns should not tempt governments to embark upon their establishment lightheartedly. Unless, as already mentioned, there is some local natural resource positively requiring a town, new towns should not normally be among the early town planning measures. They should be carefully matured after study of the urban problems as a whole.

VI

A TOWN PLANNER'S APPROACH TO HIS PROBLEM

This book is intended primarily for people who will be directly concerned with the actual work on town plans. It needs to be remembered, however, that every individual planner will be working for some corporate body, either for some form of local government organisation or for some branch of the national government. Some town planners will be employed by town planning consultants in private practice, but such consultants will normally be in contractual relationship with some government body. Frequent references will therefore be made to the need of the individual planner to convince the body for which he works of the soundness of his proposals. The individual may be the chief official or consultant concerned or he may be in quite a subordinate position, but in either case it is important that from the first he should get a clear view of the conditions of his work. This means asking the right basic questions about the situation with which he has to deal.

The first question should be: why is a town plan needed? In trying to answer this the planner will find that there are two basic sets of circumstances. *Either* there has not yet been a town plan, but it has now been decided that one is required, *or* a town plan already exists, but it has been decided that it needs amendment.

The planner will be lucky, of course, if his work begins precisely when one of these decisions is made. He may well join the staff when a good deal of work for the preparation or amendment of a plan has already been done, but that will be all the more reason for taking pains to clear his mind as to why the work was started. It is all too easy to get confused as the work develops.

The reasons for the current planning activity may never have been exactly expressed by anyone concerned. Nevertheless, they can probably be deduced from a study of the situation, and this should be done, for they probably reflect the kind of anxiety which is uppermost in the minds of those responsible for town planning. These anxieties may not reflect a sound judgment on the situation, but even if the planner concludes that they show a certain amount of confusion, this will be important in deciding how to present what he himself concludes to be the principal issues.

The current concern for the preparation of a town plan may be dominated, and consequently confused, by concern with some single prominent social problem, such as housing. That particular problem may be important and serious but, just because it is attracting so much attention, other serious and important problems may be suffering from neglect. Moreover, there is a danger that preoccupation with a single problem may destroy the very foresight that is required. Valuable industrial sites may be used for housing because housing is felt to be urgent, whereas no new industry is immediately in sight. Important road lines may be built over in order to avoid the delay required for deciding future road lines. One of the planner's most important functions is to hold the balance between urgent and remoter needs. He can never be excused for failing to recognise urgent needs or to make practical proposals for dealing with them. For this purpose he may consider it wise to sacrifice certain future interests. What he must never do is to take immediate steps *without looking to the future*. To do that would be to betray his trust.

How much Control Hitherto

Having cleared his mind as to the motives for present planning activity, the planner should next seek to judge how much control has been exercised in the past over the growth of the town. This is not as simple an issue as it looks. It is not merely a question of finding out whether there has been a previous town plan and what its provisions were. In the first place, building control may have been carried out by ordinances and byelaws (the name varies according to the country) of general application. These ordinances will have had broad rather than detailed effects, but they may nevertheless have been important for good or ill in specific ways. There have been cases where the maximum permissible height of buildings in a town was determined by firefighting considerations. Thus a regulation that was not made for town planning reasons nevertheless had an important effect on the way the town developed.

On the other hand, a former town plan that was theoretically both detailed and all-embracing may not have been fully enforced, so that its formal provisions are no guide to the actual effect it had. In this, as in many other matters, the town planner must perpetually seek for reality and never be content with formal statements if they do not correspond with reality.

When the town planner has thus analysed the reasons for present planning activity and the extent of past planning control, he will be better equipped to study the life of the town, for his assessment of the spontaneous forces at work will have to take account of how far an attempt has already been made to control them.

Assessing a Town's Vitality

The town planner will naturally take careful account of the town's functions, whether it contains much industry, is an important administrative centre, includes a harbour and so forth. In doing so he should pay particular attention to what might be called the vitality of the town. He will need to get the feel of the town and in particular of the spontaneous forces at work and the directions in which they are moving.

What is here called the "vitality" of the town has several aspects. In the first place there is the question of vigour of growth. Looking at the picture broadly, one can distinguish towns which are growing at feverish speed, others which are growing less rapidly, some which are more or less stationary, and a few which are declining. Increasing urbanisation is a major factor in almost every country, so that the rate of growth of a town is very significant. Unless it is growing fairly rapidly it is probably falling behind other towns in the same country. This may not be a bad thing, but it will certainly be important for assessing the town's prospects. In most cases the town's prospects of growth will be one of the dominant factors in the town plan.

Factors of Growth

The importance of growth can be seen from a simple example. Excess of births over deaths can easily produce a natural increase of 1.5% per year. This means that many a town, even if there is no immigration, must be expected to increase its population by about one-sixth in ten years. This alone is enough to cause considerable physical disturbance, while in many towns immigration must be expected to add to this natural increase.

Sometimes town growth is due largely to a specific and easily identifiable factor, such as the development of a port or a university. It is rare, however, for the causes of growth to be completely identifiable, and very often they can only be seen vaguely. They are partly the fruits of what one might call a general vitality, made up of many small causes. It is important to understand such elusive factors, since they emphasise the extent to which a town planner cannot control what happens and must largely seek to give shape to forces which are outside his control and only partially within his comprehension. In very centralised states, with closely managed economies, the uncontrolled element in towns is naturally smaller, but it is almost never absent, because even closely organised societies cannot trace all the inter-actions and by-products of their own organisations, once the latter become numerous and complex.

Once the town planner has recognised the spontaneous vitality in a town he will need to make some estimate of its strength and durability, since these will influence his decisions about the future and have a bearing on the resources at his disposal.

Sometimes, even when a town is growing strongly, there is uncertainty about the continuation of the forces making for its growth. When Iskenderun was embodied in Turkey just before the Second World War, it was by far the best port in the whole south of Turkey and benefited exceptionally from Turkey's economic development after 1945. By 1963, however, the comparatively nearby port of Mersin had been so extensively developed that it was a formidable competitor. This was not enough to check the growth of Iskenderun, but it clearly weakened one of the main growth factors and a planner considering the future of the town was bound to take the change into account. Similar examples can easily be found elsewhere.

For example, many towns have lost one of their orginal functions. Istanbul suffered a serious blow when it ceased to be the capital of Turkey; Vienna is a classical example of a town whose growth was affected by the alteration of political frontiers. Many small ports all over the world have suffered from improvement of internal transport, which made coastal trade of less importance.

The commonest and, in many ways, the most complex case is the town which grows rapidly for several combined reasons, partly because it is the trading centre of a prosperous area, partly because communications have developed to its advantage, partly through the successful development of manufacture, partly because it has become an important administrative centre. The planner needs to appreciate the complexity of such growth and should beware of over-simplifying the picture. He must always be on the look-out for conflicting movements. Four factors may be promoting a town's growth, while a fifth is on the decline. Cardiff, in South Wales, has expanded greatly despite losing the coal export trade which was once the principal reason why it became more than a village. Bordeaux, although it is one of France's main Atlantic ports, has been falling behind other centres as a result of wide changes in the economic forces at work within France. Karachi prospered greatly as a result of the political creation of Pakistan, but is now suffering a relative loss on account of the transfer of the political capital to Islamabad.

The planner needs to study these things for the light they throw upon both needs and resources. A small, stable, active agricultural centre may present the planner with difficult problems because, as a result of modern traffic changes, it requires considerable capital expenditure but lacks the necessary financial resources. On the other hand, of two rapidly growing towns with good prospects of increasing their wealth, one may face heavy expenditure to overcome the problems of a difficult site (think of the water problems of Los Angeles), while another may present no exceptional difficulties of terrain, for example, Adana in south Turkey.

Town Problems always Multiple

The problems of towns are always multiple. The planner must therefore accustom himself to keeping several different factors in mind and weighing up their relative importance. In most countries, but particularly in developing areas, the resources immediately available for investment in towns are usually less than the needs which, like the problems, are multiple. One of the planner's duties is to weigh the priorities carefully and, by careful foresight and economical design, to ensure that the most urgent forms of expenditure are given the highest priority. If he sincerely tries to do this, he is unlikely to find himself preparing magnificent civic designs. On the contrary, he is likely to be hard at work on basic needs such as sewerage, on everyday problems such as travel to work and so forth. Nevertheless, if the towns of tomorrow are to be more glorious and to afford better opportunities for leading the good life, the town planners of today must get down to these humdrum and practical tasks. A practical basis is essential to all fine civic design.

Inadequate though the immediate financial resources may be, they can usually be expanded once the citizens understand the need and are prepared to make an effort. This means that careful presentation of the case for action is very important and raises the temptation to make it stronger by concentrating on the dramatic. It is easy for the planner to betray his trust by allowing fascinating questions such as multi-level road junctions to divert him from the humdrum question of providing enough space for ordinary people to live in and ensuring that it has streets, water and drains.

Working with favourable Forces

In addition, he must learn to work with the forces that can help him. He must perceive where favourable spontaneous developments can be facilitated, both so as to increase the town's wealth and so as to carry out the necessary improvements with a minimum participation by public finance. This is a most important aspect of the work. Voluntary investment in town improvement is not always forthcoming, nor will it always achieve all that the town planner wants, but it can be a most valuable motive force all the same.

All this may seem a far cry from the work at a drawing board which some planners feel to be the heart of their task. Nevertheless, the importance of these studies of evolution and of the forces at work can scarcely be over-emphasised. The very solidity and artificiality of a town's buildings tend to give an impression of stability, whereas the problems of town management spring from the fact that the town is, despite all physical obstacles, constantly changing. Likewise, when a town planner is at work at his drawing board he is necessarily designing something static and is liable to think too much in terms of static qualities, whereas the essence of his work is the management of the town's *changes*. It is the unstable, not the stable, which calls for his attention. His paper plans and designs are important as tols of management. By themselves they are dead – as many town plans have remained from the moment that they were drawn.

Study Opportunities

On many points the planner will find himself constrained by technical problems. An effective drainage system must take account of the fall of the land, a river crossing must recognise where conditions are favourable for the construction of a bridge. The restrictions and frustrations are so great that it is easy to think only in terms of what cannot be done, but the planner must think also in terms of what can be done and recognise where freedom of action exists, so that the choice between solutions can either be determined by questions of design or left to the decision of private individuals.

Dangers of Paternalism

Every profession has its psychological disease, and the disease to which the town planner is most liable can perhaps be described as paternalism. Most people do not think much, or at any rate deeply, about urban problems and the town planner easily feels that he alone understands them and that all wisdom on the subject therefore rests with him. The mistake he too easily makes is to overlook the problems of those who live and work in the town because he himself is not directly concerned with the carrying-on of daily activities. He is therefore inclined to take too narrow and too stiff a line with those concerned in manufacture, in trade, in the organisation and building of residential areas, or even in the promotion of commercial recreation. In thinking that these people have a narrow standpoint he may well be right. Probably their understanding of urban problems is less than his, but their understanding of their own activities (and their particular kind of service to the public) may well be greater than his. They may, for instance, have a better understanding than he has of the kind of shopping centre that the members of the public like and consequently of what kind will be most successful.

For the moment it is sufficient to stress that the town planner is not a divinely inspired schoolmaster, whose instructions should be obeyed without question. All his requirements should be practical and reasonable. The relationship between planner and planned is not an easy one. The vigorous private individual or public official, convinced that he has a good idea and anxious to realise it quickly, is not always readily convinced that he may nevertheless be a nuisance to others. Moreover, the translation of community requirements into detailed administrative rules sometimes causes the purpose of the rules to become obscure, particularly where they are concerned with effects of light and space, which many people find difficult to visualize before a building is up, rather than directed to such matters as the need for a means of drainage, which simple people can more easily understand. It is therefore all the more important that the planner should constantly remind himself of the purpose of his work and be constantly ready to explain afresh what the reasons behind his requirements are.

Town Planning not a Luxury

There is still sometimes a tendency to suggest that town planning is a luxury for developing countries and that money should be devoted to something more "practical". This is due to a mistaken association of town planning purely with its showy, if delightful, results. Town planners are suspected, and not entirely without reason, of a burning desire to create a Champs Elysées, a New Delhi, a Lincoln Centre of the Performing Arts, without a corresponding desire to prevent the creation of slums. But a far more potent reason why town planning is still thought of as unpractical is that plans are allowed to exist in a void without being used to direct and organise the community's life. Town planners are not the only people to blame for this, but they often are to blame. They have often stuck too closely to their drawing boards.

In fact, although the necessary cost of town planning is often a difficulty in developing countries, the latter are in particular need of a strong and consistent planning policy, designed to secure extensive improvements over a period. There are several reasons for this:

(a) In the near future the urbanisation of these countries is likely to be very large in proportion to their present urban populations.

(b) In most cases there has been recent urbanisation without sufficient preparation, so that there is considerable confusion, squalor and ill-health. There are therefore arrears to be overtaken and this involves urgent planning.

(c) Thirdly, the resources of these countries are low in relation to their problems and this involves careful planning if the available resources are to be used to the best effect.

Specialist Aspects

As the town planner pursues his problem he will find that he and his colleagues become involved in highly specialised kinds of work. It is very important that this specialised work should not be shut off in a separate compartment, but some of it requires separate discussion. The main features of certain subjects will therefore be discussed in the remaining sections of this chapter.

RESEARCH

It will be clear from what has been said that town planning work involves considerable investigation. If the town planner is to understand the town's problems he must collect many kinds of information and think very hard about what he can deduce from it. As regards the population of the town he must know how it has grown as a whole and try to work out how it will grow in the future. He must know how the population of each part of the town has changed and must try to find out why. He must know about the growth of industries and how they are changing. Are the units of production getting larger and why? Are they likely to become larger still? and so on.

All work of this kind is generically classified as research, and in recent years, great stress has been laid on its importance. There is no doubt that in the past many superficial judgments have been made; it is now accepted that to avoid superficiality all conclusions should be the fruit of research into the facts which concern them.

Unfortunately, this stress on "research before you decide" has tended to produce the impression that research is a separate first stage and that all conclusions, even provisional conclusions, should be put off until the research has been done. This is an error which has led to much wasted work and confusion of thought, for it is impossible to do research with a blank mind.

This point can be illustrated by considering a volume of population statistics compiled from a national census. To many people such a volume is of almost no interest, merely a collection of meaningless figures. To a certain kind of student, however, such a volume will be of great interest and he will immediately begin to seek out particular sets of figures, to compare them, to make calculations, to seek out other figures which will help him to analyse the first ones, and so on. In other words, the volume is of interest to him because he immediately wants *to ask questions* about the information which it can give him. He is, in fact, engaged in research, even if it is of quite a casual kind, and his ability to use the figures for research is due to the fact that he already has in mind questions which he wants to ask.

He may want to know, for example, which are the biggest towns in the country, then to look at their comparative rates of growth, then to consider various aspects of the composition of their populations. Have some a higher proportion of children than others? Have some got unusually high proportions of people engaged in certain kinds of employment? He will start with a few questions and the answers to these will suggest others. Sometimes the answers he finds will be unexpected and will cause him to recast his train of thought. But he can only pursue his study of the volume, however casual, because he has a train of thought and wishes to develop it.

The first point about research, then, is that it depends upon the research worker having a preliminary idea of what questions are puzzling him and what he wants to find out.

The Difficulty of asking the right Questions

It should not be supposed, however, that it is necessarily at all easy to ask the right questions. There are plenty of examples in which some at least of the right questions have proved elusive. This can be illustrated by the interesting problem of the size of households. In many western countries between the two World Wars, repeated estimates were made of the number of dwellings needed and the actual need repeatedly proved to exceed the estimate. For some time this discrepancy was not understood and then it was realised that the size of the households was changing. Whereas it had been customary for fairly large families, often including people of three generations, to live together in a single dwelling, these groups were now tending to break up. The grandparents on the one hand and the adult children in employment on the other were more inclined to seek dwellings of their own, so that eight people who had formerly occupied one large dwelling might now occupy three small ones. Thus, even where the number of people had not changed, the demand for separate dwellings had changed considerably. Once this trend had been understood it was comparatively easy to watch for it and make allowances for it, but it was not a point which would yield to the dispassionate collection of "readymade" facts, which is what some people still believe research to be. It could only be uncovered by careful thought about the situation, by noting puzzling phenomena and by trying to find new answers to them.

Importance of Recognising New Trends

This illustrates the fundamental difficulty that it is all too easy to concentrate on accepted lines of thought, whereas the solution of tomorrow's problems is likely to involve thinking on new lines and seeking new information not hitherto required, or at least not in that form. However, at the moment when the new trend of thinking ought to be started it may not yet be obvious what the problems of tomorrow are going to be.

New trends are often neglected even after they have got well started. By the third decade of the 20th century it was already clear that road transport was causing a fall in railway traffic, but the consequences of this change were rarely faced realistically, so that there was often serious delay in reorganising railways to fit their new role.

An interesting aspect of the railway situation today is that in very large cities passenger railways are becoming increasingly important, especially for travel to work, and are actually being built for this purpose when for many other purposes they are being abandoned altogether. Moreover, these new urban railways are being built despite the need to run them at a financial loss, and considerable effort is being spent on measuring the benefits that a particular railway can bring and how big a financial loss these benefits justify. The management of our cities would undoubtedly be easier today if difficult evaluation techniques of this kind had been pursued more energetically at an earlier stage.

In facing new problems one naturally tries to think in terms of new solutions, but it is important to understand how far the problem is really new and how far some features are being discounted because those parts of it are familiar. The tendency to overlook familiar features is perhaps responsible for the fact that government by city manager (instead of by mayor and council) has not been the overwhelming success that at one time, especially in the U.S.A., it was expected to be. A city manager could, it was true, sometimes provide a city with a unity of executive direction that it had hitherto lacked, but from the point of view of understanding public opinion and persuading people to accept profound and disagreeable changes, he was often in a worse position than an elected body. The diagnosis which led to the appointment of city managers had only been a partial one, and the tendency to draw broad conclusions by considering only the obvious parts of the evidence is still a danger in town planning today.

Summary on Research

To sum up the points of principle about research:

(a) Useful research is only possible when it is trying to answer specific questions arising from study of the situation.

(b) It is not easy to frame the right questions, and the first lines of enquiry may prove to be mistaken, but there is no easy way round this difficulty. The research worker must be constantly alert to the appearance of new and unfamiliar points.

(c) At certain stages, particularly when systematic planning work is just beginning, there are many new questions to be asked, and research may then bulk larger than at a later stage.

(d) But there is no stage at which research will naturally cease. Even if a moment comes when all the questions in sight appear to have been answered, the changes which are constantly going on in a town will soon raise fresh issues. It is at the moments of apparent success that it is easiest to fail to perceive a new emergency.

(e) For all these reasons research must never be a separate compartment of the planning office, retired in academic seclusion. It must be constantly in touch with day-to-day happenings and with the actual problems of management. Research often requires separate techniques, but the techniques alone are never enough.

(f) Finally, good research is dependent upon maintaining a constantly lively and enquiring mind.

Research workers in town planning must also have a knowledge of appropriate techniques. It may not be possible to have actual staff members who are equipped with all the necessary skills, but it is important to know where the necessary specialists can be obtained as occasion requires.

No attempt will be made here to discuss all the specialist techniques which are valuable in research, but some notes on the principal branches may be useful to students as yet comparatively unfamiliar with the field.

Population. – This is of great importance and even where available statistics are comparatively limited, valuable conclusions can usually be drawn. Reference has already been made to the importance of past and future growth of population and to the vital question of migration from rural areas. In addition it is important to understand the movements of population inside the town. Which are the most populous areas? which are growing most rapidly? is the population of some areas falling and, if so, why? where do newcomers to the town tend to congregate?

Related to the above questions are those regarding housing. How many dwellings does the town contain? how does the density of occupation of dwellings vary from one area to another? do the new dwellings being erected meet the needs of all groups of the population? what are the conditions of tenure? is the housing situation getting worse or better and why?

In all these matters it is important to have the services of someone trained in statistics, but he must not be allowed to trade on the prestige of his speciality and develop studies which are not of practical benefit. Specialists can never be useful unless they work very closely with colleagues of different professions, so that the different individuals share a common body of thought about how the work is developing and what is needed in order to make progress.

Economics. – It is important that the town planners should have advice on the economic working of the town and the developments both within and at a distance which will affect its economic future. Here again this involves someone with special training, but also someone who is willing to understand the information that is required for efficient town management.

Valuation. – In many spheres of town management detailed valuation problems do not arise, though the town planner will need to have a sense of the relative values of land and how they are changing. This is something which he should be able to acquire from his own experience and with which his economic advisor will be able to help him. When schemes of urban renewal are under consideration, however, both the merits and the feasibility of the scheme may turn on the changes in value which it will cause in key sections of the town; these will need to be studied closely. It is true that changes in value only reflect changes in usefulness for certain purposes. They are no more than indices. Nevertheless, they have a most important bearing upon the financial feasibility of the scheme and on the practicability of convincing owners of property affected by it that the scheme is sound. For these purposes, it is useful to have an expert in property valuation, but he must be a man who can consider hypothetical future values. If he can only calculate existing values he will be useless.

Geographical and Physical Aspects Generally. – Any qualified town planner will have been trained in the physical appraisal of areas to be planned; these aspects, referred to in many other sections of this book, will have been studied by him much more closely and he will be less in need of outside help. Even on this comparatively familiar ground, however, he must be on the watch always to adapt academic information to strictly practical ends. It is recognised that no self-respecting town planner will move without considering geological and meteorological information, but very often there is a failure to extract from the academic sources the points of practical importance. Geology, for example ,is irrelevant save insofar as it affects the suitability of the town as an area to be lived in and the requirements for good development. Many a long recital about crystalline and metamorphic rocks could be cut short and replaced by a few shrewd observations as to how the physical characteristics of the town affect daily life and the work of construction.

Discussion of the list of specialities could be continued but it would be unfortunate if, by doing so, the impression were created that there was such a thing as a regular make-up for a planning office. Much will depend upon the requirements of a particular area and much, too, on the trained individuals that are available. Two town planners working in different areas may have significantly different teams because local needs are different. The essential point is that the chief town planner should combine a sensitive feeling for information needed with a pragmatic sense of how to acquire it.

THE TOWN PLANNER'S RELATIONS WITH THE PUBLIC

Town plans naturally affect the lives of individuals in many ways. They affect, in particular, all people concerned with building; but even the ordinary man, who may have no property at all, finds his life altered by the way the town is managed. Town management affects the congestion of the streets which he frequents, the places where he can get a house, the distance his children have to walk to school, the length of his daily journey to work and so on. Naturally, he is more conscious of the inconveniences in his life than of the ways in which it runs smoothly, and this simple fact means that his normal attitude to town planning tends to be one of criticism. He thinks he sees where his needs have been neglected, but he rarely understands what planning does to make his life easier and pleasanter.

This tendency to criticism is enough to make the problem of public relations significant; apart from that, it is clearly important that the communal action reflected in the town plan should have a realistic relationship to the needs of the various groups of people who make up the community. Unfortunately, an appropriate consultative relationship is far from easy to achieve.

Difficulties of Consulting the People

There has been a good deal of facile talk about "consulting the people", the implication being that, if this is done, the people will be able to clarify their points of view, so that the town planner can then do what the people want instead of following bureaucratic ideas of his own. But there are several reasons why it is difficult to consult the people.

In the first place, they cannot be consulted effectively unless they are familiar with both the problem and the conditions which limit the possible solutions. Fair and effective presentation of town planning problems is not easy, even when it is addressed to those regularly concerned with urban management, who are consequently familiar with this type of issue. The "people", however, are a medley of individuals, many of them without experience or understanding of urban problems and dominated by a wide variety of interests. They are incapable as a body of giving a general comment on a plan because the views of different sections vary so much. This might be regarded as merely a reason for separate consultations of more or less homogeneous groups, each of which would be able to express its own point of view. However, there is still the difficulty that most of these people, although they may be very intelligent, are quite without the experience and knowledge necessary to comment usefully on town planning problems, just as the ordinary school teacher cannot be expected to make penetrating comments on commercial affairs. Even, therefore, if one can find a more or less homogeneous group to consult and can present them with a clear statement of the problems, there is no guarantee that the resulting comments will be useful. At best they may be illuminating because they demonstrate the causes of misunderstanding prevalent in that particular group.

It would be wrong to conclude from the above that the public cannot be consulted at all, but useful consultation involves great care and trouble. In the first place it needs to be recognised that town planning problems are inherently difficult to understand, so that the main issues must be very carefully presented. This will involve describing them in different ways according to the point of view and intellectual capacity of those being addressed. Certain professional and industrial groups will respond successfully to fairly technical exposition and will enter into discussion of such matters as the availability of capital for construction which the ordinary man finds remote and unreal. Other groups will be interested almost solely in matters such as travel to work which concern their daily living conditions.

Whoever is being addressed, the commonest mistake is to present the problems in the technical language which town planners use for discussion among themselves, instead of expounding them in terms which are familiar to the audience. It is always tempting to believe that one's professional jargon is essential for discussing professional problems, but this is never true when the need is to explain the problems to people outside the professional circle. To explain in ordinary language may involve considerable effort, but it is of great importance that the effort should be made.

Consultation should always be about specific issues and not a request for general comments. The person or group to be consulted must be presented with a particular issue and with an exposition of its context before they can respond with useful criticism. This may seem to be rigging the answer in advance, but in fact no other system is practicable. (It is analogous to the fact that one cannot do research in general but must prepare a programme of particular lines of research, even if later they have to be altered.) If a specific issue is presented the result may be to produce a rather wider reaction, bringing in other issues, and this will probably be fruitful; but if the issues originally raised are too wide, the discussion will become vague and barren.

Even Mistaken Criticism is Important

Deliberately arranged consultation is likely to arouse spontaneous criticism, much of which may be felt to be unhelpful and irritating because it is the result of ignorance and misunderstanding, but the planner ignores it at his peril, because it shows what people are actually thinking. Whether their thoughts are sensible or not, useful discussion can only start from that point. A great deal of propaganda has been wasted because its originators never made contact with the current thinking of those they wished to influence and thus used arguments to which their audience was deaf.

Nevertheless, however carefully a planner works on his system of public relations, the question of securing proper public understanding of town planning problems is exceptionally difficult. The problems are both complex and interlocked. Intelligent discussion therefore involves keeping a number of points in mind simultaneously, which is difficult enough to do in a limited professional society. In a broad arena (the public press, for example) it is far more difficult and is in fact rarely achieved, even in the most advanced countries. Some progress does get made in understanding planning problems, but it often comes about through an illogical process of over-simplification, which narrows the issues under discussion at the cost of partly distorting them. This is not a desirable state of affairs, but realism bids one recognise that it exists.

Summary on Public Relations

The upshot of these reflections can be summarised as follows:

(i) For the town planner relations with the public are important and must be the object of considerable trouble on his part.

(ii) Spontaneous criticism should always be noted carefully, if only because it indicates what points are causing most dissatisfaction, whether or not it is reasonable that they should do so.

(iii) In all casual contacts with the public, town planners should be as helpful as possible and should explain the practical reasons behind the regulations being discussed.

(iv) The main objects of town planning should also be broadcast in a more general way, for example by means of newspaper articles, but this is far from easy to do in a clear and practical way that will appeal to the man in the street.

(v) Individual groups should be consulted about points that specially concern them and in every case the exposition must be adjusted to the point of view of the group being addressed.

(vi) The problems should always be explained in simple everyday language, technical terms being avoided. General phrases such as "good planning standards" should also be avoided like the plague.

None of these precepts are easy to carry out and it is often difficult to see any results from this kind of public relations work, but anyone who has been associated with a large number of town plans will testify to the great value of public relations work when it is really well done.

THE FINANCE OF TOWN PLANNING

Finance is referred to in several chapters, but the subject merits separate discussion.

Both Public and Private Finance are Important

Although the city engineer and other officials concerned purely with municipal services can think entirely in terms of municipal revenues and expenditure, the town planner needs to think of the financial aspects of all the operations that go on in the city. It will be evident, for example, from Chapter VIII on "The Characteristics of Private Development", that what happens in the town will be strongly influenced by the prosperity of all private interests concerned with building. It might be thought that when these interests are prosperous and active the planner's task would be comparatively simple, but this is not entirely true, since it is precisely at such times that spontaneous physical changes in the town, i.e. changes not initiated by the planning authority, will be at their maximum. This will cause a strong demand for the extension of public services, with all the planning that must precede their installation. It will also mean rapid changes of the kind that cause traffic congestion; the planner can be involved in a good deal of work simply in advising private interests as to the best form of redevelopment of their property, so that the rebuilding will produce the minimum number of future problems.

Problems of Municipal Expenditure

Municipal expenditure in itself must be a matter of deep concern to the town planner; in every century the claims for such expenditure have made such heavy demands on the available resources that there has been difficulty in meeting them. All municipal expenditure must be drawn in the last resort from the national or local taxpayer who would not be human if he liked paying taxes. It is rarely, however, that the citizen gets a convincing exposition of what he receives for his money and of why it has to be spent. Experience shows without any doubt that, if the case is clearly stated, the goodwill of the citizen can be materially increased. In this process the town planner has a key role, since no-one else is equally well-placed to explain the problems of the town as a whole and to make clear that apparently unrewarding expenditure (in the layman's eyes) is an essential element in creating the conditions of comfort and health which the citizens have at heart.

The whole problem of town finance, however, goes somewhat deeper than these day-to-day problems. The process of urbanisation has gathered way so rapidly and is so much a major economic phenomenon in most countries that it is creating serious strains in their economic organisation. Moreover, this is occurring at a time when we have become dissatisfied with the conditions in our towns and started to recognise the need to spend more on improving housing and public services. It is only in recent years that people have seriously tried to work out how big the future expansion of the towns must be expected to be, and the unavoidable conclusions are so disconcerting that they are rarely faced realistically. Moreover, it seems regrettably true that even the rapid growth of slums and the overcrowding in many cities of the world is not yet producing the constructive reaction which the problem requires. (This is even true of cities like New York.) This failure to respond to challenge is only partly a financial one. It also reflects failure in organisation, lack of personnel and sheer lack of imagination and public spirit. However, the financial aspect is very important and there is a widespread belief that, at any rate at present, the demands simply cannot be met. How far is this the truth?

It is certainly true that we cannot tomorrow set the whole affair right by a single courageous and far-sighted decision. What is required is no less than a major reorganisation of our society which will permit substantially more of our resources to be devoted to improvement of the organisation and physical environment of our towns. Moreover, this requirement must play a considerable part in the development of aid from the richer nations to the poorer. Yet this demand for urban improvement is not the only need. It cannot, for example, be considered apart from the need to devote greater effort and far larger resources to the development of agriculture. Nevertheless, the requirements of town development must be recognised as one of the big future demands on man's energies and ingenuity.

In another sense it is far from the truth to say that we cannot do what is required. It would be almost truer to say that we cannot do what we are already doing, for advanced countries are already spending more on the organisation and development of their towns than would have been believed possible a hundred years ago. Many nations of the world are still rapidly increasing their wealth and others certainly can increase it. It must be remembered that the growth of towns, while multiplying the problems, also increases the facilities for economic development. At the very least, therefore, the resources available in principle for town development are bound to increase.

Need for Continuous Effort

But this of course does not prove that the resources will in fact be made available where they are required. This is partly a question of determination and ingenuity. Human institutions are in many ways stubborn, but they are not absolutely intractable, and we do habitually shape them to suit our needs. The tragedy is that we do not usually devote a sufficiently passionate determination to making them do what we require. Just as, in partial response to the needs, we are already spending more on town improvement, on education, on transport, than our greatgrandfathers would have believed possible, so under greater pressure we can, if we will, devote even more of our resources to these purposes.

But what is needed will certainly not be accomplished easily. Nothing at all will happen unless towns and their needs, the costs and benefits of town improvement, are studied intensively and expounded with clarity and imagination. We do not know many of the answers and we shall not find them easily, but hitherto we have made far too little effort to find them. Compare, for example, the negligible amount of work that has been devoted to the economics of towns with the enormous (and rewarding) effort that has been given to the study of trade cycles. We can hope that intensive study will produce as great benefits in the urban affairs of mankind as it has produced in many others.

Comparative and Individual Studies

Something can certainly be achieved in the study of towns as generic phenomena. Valuable studies are now being made of the characteristics of towns of various types and sizes and of the tendency for towns of certain sizes to play a dominant role in a country's development. However, solid progress with urban studies must depend upon detailed studies of individual towns, not just as they appear at a particular moment of time, but as evolving entities in the light of the management problems that they present. The physical aspects of such studies are of great importance, but they must also be worked out as financial studies of the private and public financial interests involved.

None of this, however, is of immediate help to a town planner who finds himself obliged here and now to recommend a substantial programme of expenditure, while recognising that the existing financial arrangements, provisions for taxation etc. provide very little hope of raising the money required. There is no easy anwer to this problem, and it may take a considerable time to get the right provision made, but the duration of the struggle will undoubtedly depend upon the clarity and perspective with which the financial issues are presented by the town planners. What are the principles on which such a presentation should be made? The following points are worth making.

Summary on Presenting Financial Problems

(1) The financial problem should never be presented without a background. It should never appear as a frightening series of figures detached from purpose and achievement. Newspapers often give the worst possible impression by headlines such as "100 million dollar town plan". This immediately emphasises the size of the sum involved without giving any clue as to whether it is large in relation to the problem, to the benefits or to the period of time over which it is to be spent. Moreover, any such total sum is usually made up of a series of proposals of very different character, bringing benefits of many different kinds.

(2) Accordingly, the various items in the account should be carefully broken up and grouped according to their common characteristics. In particular, routine expenditure, such as the normal minimum provision that has to be made for every building, should be distinguished from exceptional expenditure, such as major bridging problems, central improvements and the like.

(3) Where expenditure can be expected to earn a revenue sufficient to meet all the costs, this should be made clear. The prospect of revenue is not in itself a guarantee that the expenditure will not be burdensome, but it very often has this effect.

(4) Where expenditure, though not directly earning revenue, will have an important indirect economic influence, this should be made clear, even if this can only be done by cross-reference to a full discussion of the matter elsewhere. This is still an incompletely explored field, but a very important one.

(5) Wherever possible the private side of the capital account should be shown, so that the volume of capital being served by the public expendi-

ture can be properly appreciated. Few people have any idea what large amounts of capital are already invested in towns. Apparently big increases in investment may be in line with much that has already been happening.

(6) Future expenditure should never be related simply to present values, but should be seen in the light of future growth and expected future values. This is particularly important at the present period in which many towns are growing rapidly, so that with sound management a town's assets may be expected to increase.

(7) Proposals for raising new revenue should be presented with the utmost care, so as to make quite clear their effect on various categories of people. A new charge that sounds oppressive may prove to be quite insignificant when the actual payment is worked out. The fact must be faced, however, that good future towns are bound to involve substantial contributions by the citizens.

(8) It may sometimes lend added force to the argument if the consequences of not spending money are stressed: the continuance of known health dangers, for example, or overcrowding of schools with adverse effects on the welfare of the children.

(9) Parallel examples can sometimes be quoted to show that the same kind of expenditure has been made elsewhere with success. However, the parallels must be genuine. If the likeness is only superficial the comparison will do more harm than good, but sound comparisons can be drawn.

Land Values

A word should be said here about land values. The ownership of land has often been associated, rightly or wrongly, with ideas of monopoly and oppression. In some quarters, therefore, there is a prejudice against using land values as a factor in reaching planning decisions. There is a feeling that values are only high because someone is extracting more income than he should from the land. Primarily, however, land values are always a reflection of the competition that exists for the land. This is particularly important when comparing different sites. The fact that prospective developers are willing to pay more for one site than another should never be a sole or conclusive reason for deciding future use. Nevertheless it is a factor which should not be ignored, for it shows, among other things, what people are wanting.

Certainly, high land values are sometimes the result of irresponsible profit-taking, but frequently the "profiteers" concerned are simply seizing an opportunity to sell advantageously and are not taking part in a deep-laid plot to fleece the man in the street. It is important to realise, moreover, that such opportunities to sell at high prices only exist because they reflect a high and unsatisfied *demand*. Part of the remedy for high prices, therefore, must lie in creating a supply that will meet the demand on advantageous terms from the buyer's point of view. This is likely to involve a surprising amount of work, since it is never enough to market land cheaply. It must also be accessible and provided with at least a minimum of services. This may involve new access roads and, in addition to a water distribution network, may necessitate the laying of mains from a distance. An effective change in the supply of land may therefore take a considerable time to bring about. Some facilities can be extended quickly. Others, such as trunk sewers, cannot be altered or provided without lengthy preparation.

Where land speculation and profiteering are prevalent the problem may justify amendment of the law of the land with regard to the making of unreasonable profits. This depends very much on local conditions and traditions and the problem is too complex for discussion in the present book. Such legal remedies, however, are bound to be useless *unless the unsatisfied demand is also met.*

Moreover, it is reasonable to say that the extent of "criminal" land speculation is frequently exaggerated because few people realise what the minimum costs of making land available for building are. The land must first be acquired, and the profitability of agricultural land near towns is often so high that even the land's "existing use value" may surprise many people. The land must then be serviced, sub-divided and sold, the latter usually over a period of years. If these costs are worked out on the basis of what a municipality (were it to undertake such an operation) would have to charge in order to cover its costs (including the "waiting costs" while plots remain unsold) the minimum selling price will often prove nearer to the open market price than would have been expected.

Land values are a potent source of controversy and there is little sign of a growing consensus as to how they should be treated in law and taxation. To go far into the subject here would therefore be to start a fruitless controversy. Nevertheless a few points may be made which have a practical importance.

Land Values and Public Pricing Policy

A fundamental point of dispute is how far it is reasonable for anyone, including a public authority, to charge more for land for purposes for which the demand is high. Some people hold that all profits derived from site value are "unearned" and therefore unjustified, though there is a simultaneous tendency to feel that such profits can be reasonable *if* they accrue to the public authority as representative of the public at large. The hard fact remains, however, that if land is sold at a minimum price, irrespective of demand, the effect must be to subsidise those activities which are able to use land intensively. Such a subsidy may be desirable. The point is that it should not be applied indiscriminately and unwittingly. Moreover, if demand is not allowed to reflect itself in land prices, other standards have to be found for measuring the distribution of demand and this is extremely difficult to do efficiently. It is also very difficult to secure economical use of scarce land that has exceptional site advantages if the users are not subject to the stimulus of having to pay a high price for their sites.

Town planners working in developing countries, particularly in towns where there is still plenty of scope for expansion, should not be unduly influenced by the methods and costs of the advanced countries. In countries like the U.S.A. and Germany, where the cities are already developed to a high density but are nevertheless experiencing great intensification of previous traffic levels, much attention is being given to "multi-level" development, not only at road junctions but also over considerable parts of the central area. In these highly developed countries this is both a necessary development and one whose costs, if not attractive, are at any rate less unattractive than those of alternative solutions. It is very doubtful, however, whether most towns in developing countries should follow the same line, at any rate in the 10 to 20 years immediately ahead. Sooner or later these towns must expect much more intensive development and should try to avoid intermediate solutions which would hinder it, but the costs of construction in the next few years should not be inflated by following a fashionable trend towards multi-level development. Even in the developed countries the pressure of costs may yet produce a reaction towards simpler solutions in certain cases. This is still essentially an area of experimentation.

VII

TOWN PLANNING AND THE LAW

Effective town planning must have the backing of law. It is bound to involve regulation of the activities of individuals and the town planning authority must therefore have power to compel an unwilling individual to comply with its requirements. On the other hand, the individual needs the security of knowing that the town planning authority is acting within a framework of law, so that its requirements will not be arbitrary. Town planning also involves the purchase of private property for public purposes, either for the installation of services or for the execution of public improvements. For this it must have the necessary legal authority subject to reasonable requirements to pay compensation. (The situation is not so very different if the land concerned is already owned by some other public organisation and not by a private owner. The town planning authority must still have authority to take it over and use it and in certain circumstances will be obliged to compensate the former owner.)

The use of law for this kind of community management is not new. There has been some regulation of this kind in virtually every community for centuries, but only recently have attempts been made to extend it or systematise it, so that it will deal adequately with modern urban conditions. Meanwhile many towns are becoming more and more chaotic and squalid, because systematic regulation is not available.

Common Defects of Existing Law

Unfortunately there are still many countries in which town planning law is seriously defective, the most common defects being as follows:

(i) Very often there is no comprehensive legal code, so that the erection, siting and use of buildings can only be controlled to a limited and unsatisfactory extent.

(ii) Where the law is reasonably comprehensive it may be broken up into illogical blocks, difficult to administer with the necessary elasticity and in proper co-ordination with each other. The zoning laws of the

United States, once an important innovation, are now often a hindrance to good town management because they are too rigid and also divorced from other forms of town regulation.

(iii) The administration of town planning law may be illogically divided between different agencies. In one country the agency responsible for authorising the subdivision of land into building plots (which there entails authorisation of the erection of buildings) is separate from, and unco-ordinated with, the municipal authority responsible for providing the necessary public services.

The Necessary Legal Basis

The necessary legal provisions have three main parts:

(a) Power for the government to settle what plan (which means what policy) shall be followed in managing the town, and to confer on the town planning authority the necessary responsibility and directions for carrying the policy out.

(b) Power for the town planning authority to control new buildings and uses of land so that they comply with the planning policy in the necessary respects.

(c) Power for the town planning authority to execute works of construction (such as new roads, sewers etc.) or of demolition (such as removal of unhealthy or obstructive buildings) for the purpose of ensuring proper management and development of the town.

It is important to remember these relatively simple objectives, because the detailed work involved becomes complex and can easily obscure the ultimate aim.

Adoption of a Town Plan

However good a town plan is, the mere fact that it has been prepared gives it no force as a basis for management and control. The first step required for its realisation is that it should be approved and formally adopted as the basis of management in the area to which it applies.

This basic approval of a town plan is normally carried out by some department of the central government or, in a federal state, by the government of one of the federated units. The government in question may, of course, act by means of a minister or a commission with special responsibilities for planning. This approval is usually given by the government because impartial judgment of the merits of a town plan requires action above the municipal level at which the plan will have to operate, and as free as possible from local pressures. Moreover, reasonably uniform criteria should be applied to all town plans of any single country.

This involves the question of exactly what it is that is the subject of approval. Sometimes a town plan has been drawn up in the form of a complete legal document, with a map or maps appended, the whole constituting a detailed code of regulation for one particular town. Sometimes the approval has been attached simply to a map, though that is rarely satisfactory because no map can, for this purpose, be wholly self-explanatory. The problem of the best form must depend a good deal on the details of the law in the country concerned. It will be a help, however, to look more closely at the fundamental requirements:

(i) The best policy for the future having been thought out (this is the quintessence of a plan), assurance must be provided that action over a period will be consistent with this policy. This involves stating the essential points of the policy in broad terms so that there is sufficient flexibility in minor matters.
(ii) The town planning authority administering the plan must be given the necessary power to compel individuals to comply with it, and must also be itself constrained to follow the basic policy of the plan. This entails a measure of supervision of the town planning authority by the central government.
(iii) Reasonable security must be given to members of the public who undertake development in the area. A developer who is preparing a project in order to submit it for approval must feel able to work out a plan which, while serving his own purposes, is likely to be accepted by the town planning authority. The law must make possible good flexible local administration.

To achieve the right combination of flexibility with legal force is not easy, particularly in countries with fairly simple legal and administrative systems. The task will be easier, however, if the plan is presented in the form advocated at the end of this book (see Chapter XV "Synthesis of an Overall Policy") since this should emphasise the essential points of the plan and prevent excessive concentration on legalistic detail.

Government approval involves critical assessment of the merits of the plan. This is not a legal process, but the final decision must have legal force because it will involve endorsing solutions proposed by the plan for conflicts between public organisations and private individuals or between different public organisations. As far as possible such conflicts should naturally be resolved by agreement, in other words by a reasoned discussion of the merits, but there must be no doubt about the power of the government to enforce the view which it ultimately decides to take.

In practice the settlement of such disputes involves some procedure for hearing objections to the solution proposed in the town plan. As every town planner soon finds out, problems often admit of more than one solution, and one's view of what is the best solution often depends on where one's interest lies. A builder, and also the Minister concerned with building, will be concerned with the protection of land which contains gravel or brick clay, so that those materials may be dug and used for building, where an industrialist – and the Minister for Industries – or a housing co-operative – and the Minister for Housing – may be anxious that those deposits should be built over to provide convenient sites, the necessary building materials being found elsewhere. The private individual, in differing from the town planner, is not necessarily pursuing his private interests only. He may be raising objections which are also of public interest. Accordingly, there can be no guarantee that even the most careful judgments of the town planner will or ought to be those finally accepted.

If the Government decides that an objection is valid and that the town plan must accordingly be altered, this involves having a procedure for altering the plan and afterwards confirming the amended version. The whole procedure is far from easy to devise satisfactorily. If it is too short it can be brusque and unreasonable, with the possible consequence of raising a volume of opposition which makes subsequent detailed administration extremely difficult. If the procedure is too long it can be burdensome, even to those who wish to benefit from it by making objections. This is a powerful reason for trying to ensure that the town plan is thoroughly understood and, as far as possible, agreed to by all those concerned, so that the machinery for settling disputes needs to be used as little as possible.

Day-by-Day Control of Building

Once the plan has been adopted, the conclusion follows that it must be observed, and this leads to the need for continuous control. This is not really a new need, but only the systematisation of requirements that existed already, just as town planning is not the beginning of town management but the systematisation of partial controls that have been long carried on.

No municipal government can function efficiently unless it has a good deal of systematic knowledge of the town. At the very least it needs to know how many buildings there are, how many are built or demolished each year and what each is used for. (This is to ignore, for the moment, the need for knowledge about the town's population and its distribution.) In practice, of course, even in fairly advanced countries, many municipal governments have never functioned efficiently by modern standards; one important reason for this is that they have never known enough about their towns to be clear what the needs were. The recognition of this inefficiency and confusion is one of the strongest forces behind the present-day town planning movement.

Enforcement of a town plan involves the following requirements.

Every individual wishing to put up a new building must, before doing so, submit a plan of it to the town planning authority who may require him to alter it if it does not fit in with the town plan, including detailed regulations with regard to height, distance from other buildings etc. The building as actually erected must conform with the approved plan and this means that the building must be inspected in the course of construction. If necessary, action must be taken to stop departures from the approved plan, which implies a drastic power to demolish offending buildings and impose heavy fines on offenders.

The submission of plans in this way has often been used for the additional purpose of ensuring that the structure of the new building is sound. Many people argue that the question whether a building is structurally safe is the most fundamental point about it, but this is not altogether true. If a bad building has been erected on a good site, it can be replaced by a better structure and it can be provided with public services. But if a building, good or bad in structure, has been erected on a bad site, then the whole arrangement is unsound and the only real remedy is demolition and re-erection elsewhere. Control of siting can therefore be regarded as the most important control of all.

The *geçekondu* or "mushroom houses" at Ankara in Turkey are a good example of the importance of siting. As part of the process of evading the law, many of these shacks have been erected on very steep and irregular slopes. The shacks are so numerous, and in many cases so solid, that there can be no question of their demolition at present, but it is physically impossible to provide many of them with a proper water supply, with drainage or with vehicular access. However, elsewhere in the same city *geçekondu* that are equally illegal and structurally no better have been erected on sites which do not present the same physical difficulties, so that, if their structures can be improved, they can be provided with services.

It should be noted, however, that effective control of siting does not consist simply in preventing people using unsatisfactory sites. The trouble at Ankara was not simply that people wished to evade the controls on structure, it was also that they found difficulty in getting good sites on which to build. Good siting control must therefore include making sure that a sufficient supply of suitable land is readily available.

In one respect the control of use of both land and buildings is easier than the control of building construction. With control of use it is easier to employ broad permissions, authorising appropriate types of activity in defined areas, subject only to detailed control of any construction involved. As far as possible town plans should always be drawn so that people know what liberty they provide as well as what restrictions they impose.

In the above description it has been tacitly assumed that private individuals do submit proposals for development, and this involves the further assumption that they are able to obtain land for the purpose. In commenting on the *geçekondu* at Ankara, however, reference was made to difficulties in the supply of land. The owners of the land may be either entirely unwilling to sell it, particularly for certain types of development, or they may be willing to sell only at an unreasonable price. To meet this kind of difficulty the town planning authority must have power (probably dependent upon central government approval for its use) to purchase land and make it available for development. This is most likely to be necessary for industrial zones and for the purpose of making large numbers of low-cost housing plots available. Public improvements in built areas may also involve purchase of sites by the new municipality, but this is a more specialised type of operation.

However carefully it is organised, the continuous control required by town planning demands considerable skill and a fair number of personnel. This is one reason why some people argue that town planning is a luxury which poor countries with very simple administration simply cannot afford. In a poor country simple methods must be used, even if there is some loss of efficiency, but there is a limit below which town management cannot be allowed to fall without serious consequences which are cumulative in their effects.

At present town management often falls below this level, with the result that in many cities there are areas of squalor, confusion and ill-health. Town planning is an attempt to prevent such confusion and squalor from occurring, but it cannot be a magic wand. It must have a solid basis of administrative organisation, and the creation of an adequate organisation should have high priority from the very first. Once a suitable organisation has been created it will have a good deal of work to do and the task will be a continuing one.

Interim Control

It takes considerable time to prepare a town plan and life does not stand still. The townspeople will go on putting-up new buildings and starting new activities while the planners are at work. Some form of interim control is therefore necessary, the details of which vary from country to country in accordance with local law. Whatever the legal details, however, it is essential that the town planner should see quickly where a few vital issues lie, otherwise no steps can be taken to safeguard them. It may be vital, for example, to keep certain routes open which will otherwise be closed by piecemeal action.

Execution of Works

The third legal power referred to at the beginning of this chapter is one to enable the town planning authority to execute works for the realisation of the town plan. In part these will simply be ordinary public works governed by the general law on these matters. Some of the works, however, are complicated by the need for demolition and replanning. These problems are referred to in the section on "Internal Improvements".

VIII

THE CHARACTERISTICS OF PRIVATE DEVELOPMENT

Any attempt to define the nature of a "town" easily bogs down in a philosophical description which is of very little value for practical purposes. Nevertheless certain aspects of a town can be clearly distinguished, if not exhaustively described, and it is important that the town planner should be aware of these.

A Town is made up of Individuals

Fundamentally, a town is a collection of "individuals", who have many economic and social links (it is these which cause them to constitute a town), but also act in many ways independently and therefore to some extent unpredictably. Some of these individuals are engaged in commerce, some in manufacture, many in services. These services may be professional, such as those of a banker, or quite humble, such as those of a servant in a house. A large proportion of the townspeople are engaged in "directly" economic activities, but some, such as school-teachers, are not. A minority of the individuals take part in the construction and alteration of buildings and are frequently referred to as "developers". The peculiar nature of the economics of buildings and the nature of the demand for them cause the developers to react in accordance with certain broad principles.

There is a fairly clear distinction between these individual activities and the communal activities which result from the association of so many people in a limited space. The communal activities are due to the need of individuals for certain common services and certain common regulations, so that the whole communal aspect is dependent upon the existence of individual activities. The two cannot be considered apart.

In the second paragraph the word "individual" has been put in quotation marks because the individuals in question are not necessarily single men and women. They include various forms of private organisation and also certain public organisations carrying out functions similar to those of private individuals and organisations. A public organisation, even though owned by the Government, is not necessarily carrying out government functions. A publicly owned bus company, for example, has much more resemblance to a private bus company than it does to a government tax office or education department. The phenomenon of private development with which this chapter deals, must therefore be interpreted to include some activities of public organisations.

The position might appear to be different in a highly socialised state where most or all building is carried out by various forms of public organisation. The distinction still needs to be made, however, for while the functions of some of these organisations would be regarded in any country as government work, others have functions which are not essentially governmental and in some countries these are carried out by private companies or individuals. Current language does not really possess a convenient pair of terms for the two different kinds of activity. In this chapter it has accordingly been necessary to define "private development" in a particular way.

The Definition of "Private Development" in this Chapter

From the point of view of town management:

(i) an individual wishing to build a shop;
(ii) three lawyers in partnership wishing to build an office;
(iii) a joint stock company wishing to build a shop, a hotel, a flour mill or a cinema;
(iv) a state tax department wishing to build a local tax office;
(v) an association of cattle-breeders wishing to build a cattle-feed warehouse;
(vi) a state electricity authority wishing to build a sales room and office,

are all equally "private" because they are all seeking facilities for their own activities as opposed to trying to organise the town as a whole. They all differ, but their differences only partly depend on differences of organisation. The individual under (i) may be a wealthy and competent merchant with a wide range of activities, or he may be a small man setting up in business for the first time. The joint stock company in (iii) may be very inexperienced and small in resources. The mere fact that it is a company does not make it large and sophisticated. It can even happen that the local staff of the tax office, despite belonging to a public organisation, show less understanding of town planning problems than the merchant in (i), for a successful merchant needs to observe very carefully the community in which he works. In the present chapter, therefore, the term "private" is used to cover the activities of this whole range of persons and organisations who wish to provide accommodation for their own activities.

Developers

As already remarked, by no means all the inhabitants of a town ever take part in "development", that is to say, most people never build anything, or convert a building or start an outside activity which uses a material amount of space. Most people are wage or salary earners who occupy a workplace without ever making one, and live in a house without ever building or altering one. Even if they run their own enterprises they often depend upon others for the actual provision of buildings. There is, however, a small but significant group of people (referred to above as "developers") who are investors in real property. That is to say that they are people who, for one reason or another, erect buildings either for their own use or for that of others. The make-up of the group varies from one country to another. In some countries it includes many private individuals, while elsewhere it consists largely of different kinds of public organisation. To some extent private individuals and public organisations tend to act differently in investment matters, but this is not an invariable rule, and there are certain basic similarities between them.

Although the individuals and organisations who actually undertake development are normally only a minority, they are very much influenced by the point of view of the majority. In constructing buildings the developers are often hoping to let or sell them to other people. They therefore study carefully the purposes for which buildings are needed and try to produce buildings that are attractive to a wide range of users. It will be seen below that they are more successful at this in some directions than in others.

The Profit Element in Development

For certain purposes these various types of "individual" can be classified as profit-seeking or non-profit-seeking, but for planning this is too superficial a distinction. They all, to some extent, study the prospective return on their investment, and the differences between them lie largely in the manner of their doing so. The tax department for example, does not expect to make a "profit" on its office in any simple sense of that word, but it will look carefully at the office's cost in relation to the number of people who can work in it and the amount of revenue which can be collected through it. The tax department, however, will feel able to compel its "customers" to come even to an inconvenient office and will not be afraid of "losing" them. The shopkeeper, on the other hand, cannot be sure of any customer. He must attract every single one and is therefore intensely conscious of the trade possibilities of a site. He may be much more willing than many other tenants to pay highly for a site because he foresees a heavy turnover if he can use it, but his willingness to do so will depend very much on the nature of his trade. Some traders, such as the sellers of drinks in hot climates, are extremely dependent upon having a large number of passing customers and will pay heavily for an appropriate site. The seller of pianos, who needs much space and depends hardly at all on impulse buying, will seek a site where he can pay much less per square metre. Jobbing printers and offices which do contract typing must be near their customers and easy to reach, but cannot afford to pay highly. In consequence, many such firms are found on the margins of busy areas, down the side streets of the business quarters and installed in the older, cheaper buildings.

The Time Element in Profit

In some ways, then, the various developers and entrepreneurs have a fairly sharp eye for the financial return on their place of business, whatever their occupation. When one comes to consider the time element, however, their point of view proves to have interesting limitations, partly because they do not find it worthwhile to look more than a certain distance ahead or to consider more than a limited range of possibilities.

Problems of Investment in Buildings

To understand this one must appreciate the difficulties of investment in buildings. Capital is always difficult to obtain, the returns on it are uncertain and, because buildings are so durable, efficient management requires the owner to consider a very long period. This is evident if one considers the simple question of maintenance and repairs. For about the first ten years of its life a modern building requires very little repair. Nevertheless, the wise course is to set aside regular sums every year against future repairs because, when they become necessary, the sum required will usually be larger than can be met out of current receipts. These regular allocations for repair are difficult to provide, because in this early period the owner of the building is usually anxious to repay a loan on it. In every country, therefore, some owners fail to make the far-sighted provision that they should. This enables them for a time to place fairly large sums to loan repayment or profit, but is apt to cause difficulties when the building requires to be modified to suit new requirements, since there is a shortage of cash just when it is needed. This kind of difficulty is by no means confined to private individuals and firms, but often affects the actions of public organisations and government departments.

In short, those who invest in buildings do not, at the moment of investment, usually take into account the whole life of the building. Often they are primarily concerned with the return expected on the building over the first ten or fifteen years. The value of the building after this initial period is not entirely disregarded, but the crucial factor which determines whether a building is erected or not tends to be its prospective profitability in the early period.

Obsolescence of Buildings

Another form of uncertainty is also important. The *need* for a building of a particular type may have no relation to its durability. This is particularly the case with commercial buildings and specialised industrial buildings. Nevertheless, for most purposes, it is not easy to build "short life" buildings. The following are examples of this kind of trouble:

(i) the factory which becomes too small for modern processes, but cannot be extended because it is hemmed in by other buildings;
(ii) the specialised factory building, only usable for one process, which becomes obsolete;
(iii) the shop which is too small for the modern scale of business;
(iv) the warehouse ill-adapted to modern methods of storing and moving goods;
(v) the large house, formerly occupied by well-to-do people, which comes to be occupied by several poor families.

In most of these cases (but rarely in that of the very specialised factory building) it may be possible to find a new use for the building, probably with a certain amount of adaptation. This is particularly true of the large family house, though its conversion for use by several families will only be satisfactory if separate washing and cooking facilities are provided for each family. On the other hand the new use may be only a second best. The small factory may continue in use, but inefficiently and at a very low rent. A warehouse may even be turned into unsuitable dwellings if the pressure for living space is strong enough.

In the most favourable circumstances, the demand for really good accommodation is so heavy that an obsolete building is quickly demolished and replaced by a first-class building of a different kind. This happens in only a minority of cases, because the demand for buildings, especially cheap buildings, is usually so great (as a result of the rapid growth of towns) that it tends to outrun the supply of new buildings. Paradoxically, therefore, a building which is no longer wanted for its original purpose and consequently falls in value may prove to be in strong demand for some other purpose precisely because it is relatively cheap. The second and subsequent users of the building are often opportunists, anxious to secure temporary accommodation, but giving very little thought to long-term maintenance. In consequence the building deteriorates.

Why Replacement of Buildings is often delayed

In theory the best course is always to provide the optimum type of building for every purpose as soon as it is required. In practice this is often impossible simply because there are so many demands on the available capital and labour. Shortage of building *labour* can often be a serious difficulty even when money is available. Attention has often been drawn to the way in which Americans tear down and replace buildings which had been erected only a few years before, but even in America this practice is limited to a few areas of specialised demand. America too has many obsolete buildings, witness the old slum tenements of New York City.

One reason why obsolete buildings are not replaced is that it is sometimes simpler and cheaper to abandon the old building and construct a new one on an empty site at the edge of the town. This can be criticised as typical short-sightedness by private enterprise, but a public authority in a similar position may take the same course since, like many a private individual, it may lack the resources necessary for pursuit of the course which is theoretically the optimum. This is not simply a question of efficiency on the part of the individual or organisation concerned. Inefficiency may be a factor, but very few communities are yet organised so as to have the optimum facilities available for both demolition and construction. Perhaps the Scandinavian countries are the only ones which can be said to be in that happy position. In most countries it is still difficult to organise the carrying-out of enough construction. Consequently, it is important not to embark on unnecessary demolition; this means that the adaptation of older buildings, even at the cost of some inefficiency, may be important. The greatest immediate benefit is sometimes to be secured by concentrating on new construction without demolition.

Slow Turnover of the Building Stock

It is a help in understanding this particular aspect of a town to realise that the total number of existing buildings is large in comparison with the number built or demolished each year. Ordinarily, therefore, a large part of the total stock of buildings cannot be changed rapidly, even if the demand for change is strong. Extraordinary measures can, of course, be taken. The rate at which buildings are erected or demolished can be increased, but such an alteration cannot be carried through rapidly because it means increasing the size of the building industry and this, apart from the complicated financial questions involved, requires the training of additional skilled labour, which cannot be done in a hurry.

Naturally the need for demolition and replacement cannot be ignored indefinitely. Moreover, as will be seen later, it is often important that the public authority should initiate the replacement process. Nevertheless, it is important to recognise that demolition of obsolete buildings is often neither practicable nor desirable.

Thus, even if failure to replace obsolete buildings to the optimum extent is often due to miscalculation by "private" developers, it may be impossible to say what the perfect course of action would have been; the errors can only be minimised by very careful study, such as the individual developer can rarely undertake. The town planning authority, however, may be able to help a good deal. It can sometimes act as an enlightened developer, partly because it has access to government sources of finance. But it will not be successful unless it studies the point of view of the private developer, because only thus will it understand the nature of private demand.

Squatting

One particular kind of private development needs special reference and that is the phenomenon commonly known as "squatting". Under modern conditions it often happens that immigrants flood into a town far faster than dwellings can be provided for them. The result is an accumulation of desperate people seeking shelter at any price and this often leads to the starting of illegal settlements. These settlements may be illegal in more than one sense. In the first place, the inhabitants may have no title to the land on which they "squat", simply defying the owners to remove them. In the second place, they may have erected buildings which do not comply with the local building control as regards either site or structure. In the simplest case the individual occupying the building has himself squatted on the plot and erected the hut. In other cases he may be renting the hut from an "owner" who has himself erected it illegally. Moreover, if the illegal settlement has been allowed to remain in existence for a long time, the original primitive huts may in part have been replaced by substantial houses of a more or less orthodox pattern.

Once illegal settlements of this kind have grown up, it is usually impossible to enforce the law by ejecting the illegal occupiers and demolishing the dwellings for the simple reason that the occupants have nowhere else to go, so that enforcement action would result in an intolerable amount of hardship. This emphasises the most important underlying aspect of these illegal settlements.

In order to understand and cope with squatting, it is necessary to realise that the fundamental trouble is the scarcity of land and dwellings obtainable on reasonable terms by the squatters. In addition, the flood of immigrants is usually unforeseen, so that necessary measures to provide what they need are not taken in time. No remedy will work unless it includes the provision of areas where immigrants can live easily and cheaply. Moreover, usually the remedy cannot be a once-for-all measure. It is not sufficient to provide alternative and better sites and dwellings for the existing squatters. The whole situation must be altered so that further waves of immigrants will not have to squat and can be guided to areas suitable and cheap enough for them. It is usually a necessary part of the remedy that the Government should revise its previous ideas about the number of immigrants to be expected and should consequently adjust upwards all the provision that is to be made for them. It must always be remembered that such immigrants are necessarily poor; if the accommodation provided for them is expensive, they are bound to refuse it and to start illegal settlements all over again.

Importance of Cheap Sites

Accordingly, the first requirement is that plenty of cheap sites should be available, each provided with at least the minimum services. Water must be provided, at least by means of standpipes, and also the minimum drainage. Electricity is likely to be the least difficulty. Schools are important and it may be difficult to find sites for them if the growth of squatters' huts has gone too long uncontrolled. The mere provision of such cheap sites (not to speak of houses) involves the planning authority in a great deal of advance work. This enhances the importance of foresight, so that unexpected changes shall not take the authorities by surprise.

Once these cheap sites are available and serviced to the minimum extent, the best answer in many places will be to encourage self-help by the occupants. In certain climates immigrants can easily supply themselves with at least the minimum of shelter, though even here regulation may be important to prevent the encouragement of pests by certain forms of primitive construction. In colder climates and those with heavy rainfall, the structures may have to be more elaborate and may require more help from the local authority. It is not the intention here to discuss the detail of how this can be done, but it should be stressed that even self-help housing cannot work satisfactorily without careful management. Moreover, standards must not be set too high, or the result will be to restrict the flow of new dwellings and to create the conditions for squatting all over again.

The main point is that squatting is always the result of inadequate supply of housing; any remedy must therefore include effective and adequate provisions in this respect. Mere plans to provide houses are not enough. All the necessary machinery must be laid on to ensure that the necessary number of plots and houses is actually produced. This may seem a hard saying because it is precisely this adequate supply of houses which is the biggest urban problem of today. Nevertheless, there is no evading this condition of success and the stark difficulty of the task needs to be recognised.

It needs to be recognised, too, that the present wave of immigrants to the towns is not going to be a temporary trouble. Reasons have been given in Chapter II, "The Present-Day Importance of Towns", why migration to the towns is likely to be an important phenomenon for many years. Many a town which is alarmed by the present volume of immigration would be well advised to prepare for an even larger volume in years to come.

Summary on Characteristics of Private Development

It will be useful to summarise the points that the town planner needs to understand about private development:

(i) It is a spontaneous activity, reflecting growth and change in the life of the community and the consequent need for buildings in which to carry on new activities. Despite certain defects referred to below, it is therefore a most important activity on which the very existence of the town depends. If private development is slow and hesitant, this is probably a sign of economic ill-health, because it means that the basic activities of the town are failing to develop. Even public organisations will not carry out development in a town regardless of the economic outlook. It is possible for a stable town to be economically healthy, but in the present phase of urbanisation this is very unusual.

(ii) In certain circumstances private developers show considerable perspicacity in judging what the community needs, but each individual developer is working separately and is liable to misjudge the general effect. For example, traffic congestion can result from a series of individuals each taking steps to extend a different building and thus increasing local activity without regard to the consequent creation of additional traffic. In such circumstances, the town planning authority must protect the individual developers from causing confusion for each other.

In recent years, a striking development in the USA has been the construction of entirely new shopping centres on the fringes of towns, which are thus easily accessible to shoppers in cars. Many of these new centres have been very profitable, but may yet suffer from too many attempts to imitate their success. This kind of excessive development needs to be restrained in the interests of developers as well as the public, but this is not easy to do.

(iii) The desire of developers to create new buildings is complicated by the availability of old buildings which have ceased to be used for their original purpose. The result is the problem of obsolescence, many buildings being used in an opportunist manner to less than their full efficiency, falling into gradual decay and creating the problems of "blighted area" and "slums" (see also pp. 96-97).

(iv) Private development (for reasons which cannot be fully discussed here) does not usually meet all the needs of a fully organised society. Further back in history, because men lived in fairly primitive dwellings, it was easier than it is now for "private development" to provide dwellings that were adequate by contemporary standards, for individual families could easily erect their own huts. Moreover, throughout the rapidly growing towns of the world, there are collections of shacks, "mushroom towns", "bidonvilles" and settlements with other names which are all a desperate form of self-help housing. They are all "private development" and in a sense they are all better than nothing, yet they are all appallingly unsatisfactory. Despite these attempts to improvise solutions, there is still a shortage of even poor quality accommodation. In the modern world private development has never, unaided, been successful in providing enough good *cheap* housing.

Private development is thus a peculiarly ambivalent phenomenon. It is a most valuable part of the life of the town and yet it often fails to meet all the community's needs. It is irreplaceable, but if it is not carefully supervised it will run wild like a weed and choke itself with its own congestion. Yet if the private developer is "supervised" too vigorously and unwisely, he is apt to conclude that regulation is making his chance of profit too uncertain and he will simply cease to build, with very serious consequences for the life of the town.

The defects of private development have led some people to conclude that it is an inherently bad thing, a form of disease which should be wholly suppressed, but this is rather like concluding that, because some men commit crimes, all men, including the policemen, should be suppressed. If the characteristics of private development are well understood, its virtues can be made use of and its vices kept in check. The art of doing this may be compared with gardening. The town planner must study the conditions of growth of all the valuable forms of development and must endeavour to create these conditions as far as he can. At the same time, he must try to cut back and control the unsatisfactory forms of growth without hindering growth in general.

Something will be said later about how the deficiencies of private development can be supplemented, but they all depend on understanding its characteristics.

The Conditions for Good Private Development

What, then, are the conditions for good and successful private development? In the first place, of course, there must be favourable economic conditions for the type of activity that the new buildings are intended to serve. That is a matter which lies wholly outside the scope of this book, but it may be useful to mention other conditions, which concern the town planner more closely. The private developer will be anxious to know what forms of regulation he will have to observe, and will not necessarily be hostile to them provided he can see that they benefit him, either directly by improving his building, or indirectly by preventing his neighbours from being a nuisance to him.

The private developer will be particularly anxious for the maximum amount of positive assurance in advance. He will want the town plan to make clear where he can pursue his particular type of activity as of right, without having to seek permission to do so. Likewise, he will want to know as far as possible in advance the detailed siting requirements that the town planning authority will impose and what structural requirements he must comply with. He will wish to know what public services will be available for his building and what he will have to pay for them.

Now it is not at all easy for even the best organised town planning authority to do all that the private developer wants in this way. A plan which leaves no questions open for settlement when an actual project is made is a rigid plan and that will not make it attractive to the private developer. For example, if the plan indicates the line of a new road, this will probably involve eventual interference with existing buildings, but it is most improbable that the exact date of construction of the new road will be known when its line has to be decided. Perhaps it will be built five years hence, perhaps ten. What, in the meanwhile, is to be done about the existing buildings? Must no alterations or additions be made, however temporary, however urgently needed? A total prohibition of this kind would have the advantage of being perfectly clear, but it would also be needlessly restrictive, and would be likely to cause resentment at the "wooden" and uncooperative attitude of the town planning authority.

The same difficulty would probably arise if an attempt were made to lay down in advance and in detail what could be done pending the building of the road. On the other hand, if the planning authority has discretion to allow certain changes conditionally, it may be possible to safeguard the line of the road without restricting too severely the interim use and alteration of the existing buildings.

How the Town Planning Authority can help Private Developers

From the point of view of the private developer, therefore, the greatest benefits do not always flow from the most precise rules, because they tend also to be rigid rules. Nevertheless, if the town planning authority once grasps the need to cooperate with private developers, it can do a great deal by approaching its administrative task in the right frame of mind. For example, it can:

(i) define areas where industrial buildings, warehouses, shops and houses respectively can be erected freely, subject to approval of structure and detailed siting (this will be compatible with having other areas where some of these types of building can be erected only with special authorisation);
(ii) define the areas where buildings may be erected at once, as opposed to others which are regarded as reserves for future development;
(iii) state clearly and carefully both the objects of detailed control of siting and also as many as possible of the specific rules which are to be applied;
(iv) state clearly in the same way the rules governing the permissible structure of buildings.

The most that can be done in this kind of way will still make it necessary to require a specific approval for each new building and each alteration of a building, though perhaps not for all changes of use of buildings or land. Careful advance statements of this kind will, however, enable the individual developer to be clear in what ways he has to satisfy the town planning authority and will make him feel that the latter is playing an intelligent and necessary role and not simply making itself a bureaucratic nuisance.

Some readers may object that the above paragraphs presuppose a rather elaborate and complex day-to-day planning administration. This is to some extent true, though the process can be simplified where the administrative resources are extremely limited. The whole operation, however, needs to be seen in the right light. The management of towns is one of the most important administrative operations of human society. Moreover, recent events have made very clear the serious evils that result from its neglect. For these reasons town administration should be recognised as something worth doing well, even at the cost of a good deal of effort. More effort and thought devoted to town planning can bring dividends which are infinitely worthwhile.

One further word should perhaps be said about the relations of the town planner and the private developer. It has already been stressed that each has good knowledge of his own sphere, but needs to know more about the point of view of the other. But if the two really understand one another they can help each other materially. The private industrialist, for example, may be able to make helpful contributions about the characteristics of traffic flows which neither party could have thought out alone. Likewise, the town planner, once he understands how the industrialist approaches his problem, may be able to help the latter over questions of industrial siting, by giving him information which the industrialist alone, lacking an overall view of the problems, could not acquire.

IX

GROWTH AND CHANGE IN TOWNS

In all countries most towns are growing, often at a speed which makes it very difficult to maintain proper control of their extension. In fact, the number of towns which are stationary or falling in population is usually extremely small. It is true that small towns often grow a good deal less rapidly than large ones and sometimes cease to be the dominant commercial centres of the surrounding areas. In some respects this is a form of retrogression and it may mean that the smaller towns are becoming *relatively* poor. That is to say that, even if income per head is rising in the small towns, it may be rising less rapidly than in the large ones; this may give the small town people a sense of losing in the race and may cause important psychological reactions. Talented young people may desire to get away from small towns to big ones where they feel that their chances are better. This cause of discouragement, however, should be distinguished from an actual fall in population and income. There is a danger that the role and problems of middle-sized and smaller towns will be discounted too much because their problems are less dramatic, and are therefore felt to be less urgent, than those of the very large metropolitan towns. Yet the dominance of metropolitan towns is causing more and more concern; there is increasing interest in decentralisation, so as to limit metropolitan growth even if it cannot actually be stopped.

Decentralisation can only be studied intelligently if there is a thorough understanding of the lesser towns and if they get a proper share of available development resources, such as money for the expansion of their public services.

Where a town shows an actual decline of population, this usually reflects a serious economic condition, probably due to the collapse of some local industry or the exhaustion of some local resource. Each such case requires careful analysis and this should be done urgently; measures of rehabilitation usually require time to become effective, so that decline may easily go a long way before it is checked. Each case, however, needs to be considered separately and the matter cannot be adequately discussed in the present book.

In most towns in developing countries the rate of growth is uncomfortably fast, even if it is well below the maximum in that country, and there is always a chance that it will become yet faster. As already noted in Chapter II (The Present-Day Importance of Towns) a natural increase (excess of births over deaths) of 1.5% per annum is quite common, and this alone is sufficient to raise a town's population by about a sixth in ten years. But, as emphasised in the same chapter, immigration from rural areas can easily be a stronger influence than natural increase. A total annual increase of 5% is quite common, which involves a population growth of two-thirds in ten years, while 8%, which more than doubles the population in the same time, is not unknown.

Importance of Forecasting Rate of Population Increase

It is therefore very important that the town planner should have a realistic view of the total rate of increase to be expected and should be careful not to underestimate it. If he overestimates, he is likely, at worst, to make a mistake in his time scale, the development that he forecast simply taking rather longer than he thought it would. But, if he underestimates, the expansion programme will be started on too small a scale and it may be difficult to secure its necessary enlargement in time. In recent years, underestimation of growth has been more common than the opposite.

Population growth is so important that serious errors in forecasting will always be a nuisance. This kind of forecasting therefore merits very careful attention and the estimates should be regularly checked against actual results.

Growth has both external and internal effects on the town, the latter being easier to understand if the results of the former are considered first. The present chapter therefore concentrates on the external effects.

External Effects of Growth

The basic problem is the physical spread of the town. Growth in population is bound to cause such a spread and it may be added to by the effects of technical changes in local industries and by a rising standard of living.

Physical Problems

Even if there are no physical obstacles the physical spread needs to be organised; in practice there are usually some complications, of which the following are examples:

(a) Natural physical features such as waterways and mountains which force growth in a particular direction and complicate the pattern of communications. Some physical obstacles are not visible and require considerable research. Examples are the existence of a high water table which makes building difficult, liability to subsidence from undergrond mining or liability to earthquakes. Apart from exceptional winds, even absence of wind can be a problem. It can have a serious effect in worsening smoke nuisances, as has happened at Ankara.

(b) Big industrial plants such as steelworks and petroleum refineries have somewhat the effect of physical obstacles, but in addition they have the quality of attracting certain kinds of movement. Where such big plants exist they constitute virtually immovable obstacles. Where they do not exist it is particularly difficult to foresee where they will be required. Sometimes it is important to leave the only possible large industrial site free, even if at present there is no prospect of a large plant occupying it.

(c) Certain areas may require to be kept in their present condition because they contain national monuments or have exceptional landscape beauty.

The object of analysing growth problems of this kind is partly to find out where difficulties exist, but it is equally important to find out where freedom for growth exists or can be made to exist. There are inevitably so many obstacles that it is valuable to know where development can be pushed ahead easily or how much freedom could be gained by a particular operation such as the building of an important bridge.

Problems due to Growth

Looking at growth problems from another angle it is worthwhile to distinguish the following points:

(i) Population increase is usually accompanied by some increase in the number of buildings, but the latter increase may not correspond with the needs, particularly where population growth speeds up rapidly. As far as certain categories of buildings are concerned, particularly dwelling-houses, one can even say that it is normal for the supply to fall short of the demand wherever a town is growing rapidly. That is one of the dominant problems of town life today.

(ii) The increased population needs increased public services, which ought to be provided in advance of the buildings. Here again one can say that it is normal for the supply to fall short of the demand.

(iii) The growth of population may make some existing services less adequate, for example by increasing congestion on the roads.

(iv) The physical surroundings of the older parts of the town may be altered by the growth of new ones outside them. The new areas may increase even more rapidly by drawing population away from older ones that are losing their amenity. New centres of shopping etc. may draw business from older areas as well as from new ones.

Thus external growth makes demands on the municipal authority for extension of existing services and may also require the provision of services of new kinds, such as low-cost housing, because former sources of supply are becoming less adequate. This provision for the needs of external growth can only be made satisfactorily if work has been begun well in advance. For sewerage and water supply, work may have to begin three to five years in advance of the time when the supplies are needed, particularly if it is necessary to develop a new source of water.

In addition, even if the extension of the town goes as well as possible, the planning authority will have to regulate land use, partly to prevent the new developers being a nuisance to each other through uncoordinated action and partly to ensure economical design of the public services. (See also Chapter XIII [Technical Aspects of Town Planning].) The planning authority can only carry out this regulation if the town planner has furnished it with a forecast of development to be expected and an analysis of how it can be distributed to the best effect.

There can be no hard and fast line between external growth and internal change in a town, particularly as some external growth is bound to result from internal changes. But then there should be no hard and fast lines in the town planner's mind. He should be able to think clearly and in detail about any single aspect of his problem without divorcing it from related aspects.

Internal change may be independent of growth. It can come about in the following ways:

(i) *Technical Innovation.* – Even though an activity is not increasing in volume, it may undergo a change of process which requires a different organisation and a different (often much larger) type of building. In many countries this will in the next 20 years be an important result of gradual replacement of artisan handwork by machine manufacture. Even where machines are quite simple they often involve a move to a workshop at least ten times the size of the old artisan workshops, few of which are more than three metres square. Usually such a change is accompanied by a move from some old part of the town to a new industrial area on the outskirts.

(ii) *Increase of a Particular Activity.* – This may be the result of a technical change such as the development of motor transport, which increases movement partly because it makes it easier. Alternatively, it may result from a rising standard of living, which enables more people to buy cars.

(iii) *Changes in Type of Building.* – This in fact is largely due to technical changes in construction, making new types of building practicable, but the speed of the change may be influenced by a rise in incomes. One obvious example is the tendency for apartment buildings to replace single-family dwellinghouses. This is particularly stimulated by growth of population causing increased pressure on central sites, but it can also be the consequence of a change of fashion once apartment building becomes possible.

(iv) *Changes in Type and Volume of Traffic.* – This is really conditioned by the two types of change referred to above, namely, technical innovation and rising incomes. Congestion of road traffic is the most frequent manifestation, but other aspects should be borne in mind. Transfer of traffic from rail to road may have an important influence on industrial siting. In many cities factories were originally sited in close proximity to the railway, whereas now similar manufacturers prefer sites giving good road connections. Decline of railway traffic may also provide opportunities for diverting some railway-owned land to other purposes.

External growth normally has certain internal effects, particularly by causing an increase of activity in the old centres. This always happens to some extent, even where new sub-centres develop as well but, particularly if external growth occurs more on one side of a town than on another, there may be a tendency for the old centre of activity to shift. The centre of activity in London has moved westwards to Westminster and in Istanbul it has moved north of the Golden Horn; in New York two centres have developed, the old financial centre in downtown Manhattan being more or less separated from the mid-town business centre around 42nd Street.

The problems raised by internal changes depend less on whether they are due to increase of population than on whether they cause increase or reduction of activity in particular areas. Increase of activity and therefore of pressure is by far the most frequent phenomenon. Widespread growth of population and rising standards of life see to that. This causes rises in price through competition for land, displacement of some activities and also various obsolescence problems due to conversion of buildings from one use to another as the predominant activity in the neighbourhood changes.

In addition, however, there may be reduction of pressure amounting sometimes to local dereliction, particularly where change is due to technical innovation rather than growth in activity. Sometimes the effects can be quite dramatic. A good example is the Landore area of Swansea, Great Britain, where, until rehabilitation recently started, a large area close to the centre of the town had become derelict and largely deserted. The effect was the more striking because the presence of metallic deposits entirely prevented the growth of vegetation on much of the land. Likewise it is evident that much of the old city of Istanbul has relapsed into relative quiescence compared with the intensive activity taking place north of the Golden Horn.

Remedies for both these types of change are discussed in the following chapter.

X

INTERNAL IMPROVEMENTS

Despite the pressures and stresses described in Chapter IX on "Growth and Change in Towns", the process often takes place spontaneously and without any direction from the public authority. This is particularly likely to happen where the private developers are intelligent and experienced and have enough land and money to rebuild their property to advantage.

The Question of Initiative by the Public Authority

But because private property is criss-crossed by public property (the streets and services alone ensure that the pattern is complex), circumstances often arise in which a sound improvement involves active participation by the planning authority. In a large proportion of these cases the improvement will not get under way unless the public authority takes the initiative. One of the town planner's most difficult tasks is to know when to intervene and try to initiate a scheme of improvement. In the first place he will be faced with the usual multiple claims on the community's resources. There will always be plenty of tasks even if no improvements are tabled at all. In the second place it is not easy to judge the optimum moment at which to make an attack on the problem, particularly as the implementation of any extensive development usually takes a number of years.

Origins of Improvement Problems

In order to give some guidance as to how these problems are best tackled it will be best to analyse the main reasons for improvement.

Internal improvement problems, despite their innumerable forms, fall into two broad categories

(a) those arising from congestion,
(b) those arising from decay and under-use.

As far as congestion is concerned, traffic hold-ups are one of the surest signs of trouble of some kind, but they do not necessarily indicate a need for physical reorganisation of streets and buildings. Incipient traffic congestion can often be eased by good traffic discipline, by the prevention of indiscriminate parking, and by such measures as the reorganisation of public transport termini. Moreover, growing congestion may sometimes be eased by natural changes such as the growth of a new shopping centre in another part of the town.

The Reasons for Congestion

Nevertheless, the appearance of traffic congestion, even if it can be successfully dealt with, is usually a sign of increasing pressure in the neighbourhood and may well reflect a trend that will cause difficulties sooner or later.

Occasionally traffic congestion is caused by drivers trying to pass through an area rather than do business there; they will be glad to take advantage of a by-pass, if one is provided, and there is no need for reorganisation of local activities. Far more often, a proportion of the vehicles have business in the area and the congestion is primarily due to the attempt to carry on a great deal of activity in a very restricted space. The real causes of the trouble must therefore be sought in the changes of activity which have led to the increase of traffic.

How a Small Town Grows

The way in which congestion grows can be understood by following the growth of a small town as its business expands. At first there will probably be a single business street, or at most two intersecting each other. Commercial buildings and dwellings will be mixed up together, and commercial buildings may also be mixed with artisan workshops. The buildings will be low and may not occupy a very large proportion of the plots on which they stand, though the frontage buildings are likely to be fairly continuous.

As the town grows and business expands, the following changes will tend to take place:

(i) the number of people and vehicles frequenting the street will grow;
(ii) the buildings will get larger and more specialised: dwelling-houses and workshops will move out of the busiest areas, new institutions such as banks will move in, certain types of trade will move to the cheaper sites on the fringes;
(iii) the buildings will get larger, occupying more of their plots and increasing, at least in some instances, the number of storeys;

(iv) the commercial centre will start to spread, with the result that what used to be minor roads and even alleyways will become busy trading streets without being widened to suit their new role.

The result of all this will be that the roads become much busier and congested. Moreover, the extension of the commercial area to the side streets is likely to complicate the traffic pattern and worsen the congestion. This state of affairs suggests the simple conclusion that the streets should be widened. However, because the buildings fronting the streets become more solid and more expensive with increased activity, street widening becomes more difficult. On the other hand, the redevelopment of the original buildings has probably extended to the street frontages only, so that much back land is difficult of access and cannot easily be used for the rapidly growing needs. One sees here the short-sightedness of private enterprise, which very often does not look far enough ahead to make the optimum use of its own property; to be fair, however, both public and private developers often have to take a shortsighted course because at the crucial moment they lack the resources to do otherwise.

Possible Forms of Improvement

When congestion of this kind arises, the simplest possible alteration, in one sense, is to demolish one side of the street, set the buildings back and rebuild, thus leaving the whole situation as it was before, except that the street is wider. Sometimes this really is the simplest solution, especially if the town is not very large and complex, the buildings to be demolished are not very valuable and there is plenty of spare space behind them on which to rebuild.

But very often this is not a simple solution at all, one quite common difficulty being that it may not be easy to set the buildings back without disturbing another and important land use, perhaps commercial buildings which front on a neighbouring street. At best, moreover, a simple widening of this kind is largely a prolongation of the existing situation. It may work quite well if it is a once-for-all alteration, but will it be? If growth and change have produced congestion once, will they not continue and create a fresh set of complications in only a few years?

For reasons of this kind, the town planner often tries to bring about a more far-reaching improvement, which looks further ahead and tries to take advantage of the trends that have been established. Reference has already been made to one such trend: the growth of specialisation. The main street of the original small town was an all-purpose area, where all kinds of business were done and where many people lived, while at the same time it was a means of communication. As the town grew, the businesses in and around the street gradually sorted themselves into groups and competed rather inefficiently with one another for space, the main reason for inefficiency being the "stiffness" of the whole lay-out, the difficulty of moving buildings or even of cutting new accesses through them. At the same time, the mere growth of the town increased the traffic in the street. The traffic directly associated with the activities of the street grew more intensive while more vehicles from other parts of the town simultaneously wanted to use the street as a means of communication.

The broader and far-reaching improvement schemes vary greatly in detail, but they usually try to take advantage of trends of the above kind and also of the general tendency to growth. First, they try to separate out the through traffic, giving it an easier route that will encourage it to avoid the business area which it has no need to penetrate. Second, the whole lay-out is revised so as to provide more room for expansion and to adjust the road system to the new needs. Third, specialisation is carried further, businesses being grouped still more conveniently, while bigger and more carefully designed buildings provide more accommodation in a small space, but with easier communication both within and between the buildings.

There is no fundamental difference between improvement schemes of this kind for big towns and for small ones, but in big towns the congested area tends to be larger and more complex and the shifting of any element in the area more difficult. Buildings are larger, values higher, and one has to go further afield to find a relatively clear space. Consequently, analysis of the problem tends to be much more difficult. The working-out of suitable methods of analysis is one of the main preoccupations of town planners today. The solutions also tend to be more difficult and lead *inter alia* to devices such as elaborate underpasses and two-level roads. There is a danger in such circumstances that too much attention will be concentrated on the elements in the problem which are easily calculable, such as traffic flows, and too little on the changes in use and habits which are the fundamental influences. Likewise, it is easy to think too much in terms of engineering solutions such as underpasses and too little in terms of re-organisation of the activities that they serve. Purely engineering works certainly play a very important role in the big cities of today, but the purpose which they are intended to serve must always be worked out carefully and they must always be seen in relation to other parts of the town.

Conditions for a Successful Improvement Scheme

No attempt will be made here to discuss the details of such schemes, which could quite well occupy a separate book of their own. It is important, however, to understand some of the problems and principles involved. Schemes of this kind can be extremely successful and will be increasingly necessary as our towns continue to develop, but if they are to be successful certain conditions must be fulfilled:

(a) The improvement scheme as a whole may eventually be profitable, but in the meanwhile it will certainly require a great deal of money. Apart from the demolition of buildings and the construction of new ones, the roads and other public facilities generally have to be made more elaborate and expensive. The financial problem must therefore be considered from the first and it has two aspects. One is to make sure that plenty of capital is available for the necessary rebuilding (which means available to both private and public organisations). The other is to be sure that the capital is applied advantageously, which implies very skilled assessment of the usefulness and practicality of the new layout.
(b) Even if the improvement is carried out rapidly by the standards of such operations, it will be spread over quite a period of years. The scheme must therefore be designed as one that can be carried out in stages.
(c) The scheme must command the confidence of a large number of people, particularly all those whose investments are required in order that it may be realised. This means a great deal of persuasion and convincing exposition.
(d) The scheme must be designed in such a way that it can be carried out while the life of the town continues. This very often adds seriously to the technical complexity of the operation.
(e) There must be consistent, farsighted and intelligent management.

This means, of course, that the scheme must have a utilitarian aspect, but not that it need be mean or dingy or *solely* utilitarian. While it is one of our objects to make towns pleasant and cheerful places to live in, they will not exist at all unless they are alive and work efficiently. No concern for "higher spiritual values" should therefore cause the purely practical side to be neglected.

To fulfil the conditions set out above, it is of the greatest importance that the reasons for the scheme and the nature of the solution proposed should be set out in writing with great precision (a map alone is never adequate). This very careful exposition is necessary if the town planning authority is to make a sound judgement on the scheme. It is also a prerequisite of convincing the various people and organisations that will have to invest in the scheme. Finally, it is important for maintaining consistent management of the scheme over the whole period of its execution. It is by no means easy to ensure that complex schemes of this kind are discussed broadly and thoroughly, and it is more difficult to ensure this if the exposition is not done very carefully.

Schemes for Blighted Areas

In the light of this brief description of what might be called the "de-congestion" type of scheme, one can the more easily understand the other main type which aims at the revival of blighted areas.

The kind of area that is commonly called "blighted" has undergone some kind of decline and is showing no sign of recovery. It is a symptom that the economic system of a town is imperfect and does not manage to make the optimum use of its assets. A blighted area is not simply a slum area, for the latter, despite its bad housing conditions, can sometimes be lively and vigorous and rapidly evolving. The essence of a blighted area is that its original activity has declined, so that it has become poorer. Its buildings, in part at least, have lost their original purposes, so that they are used in a makeshift and inefficient manner, are badly maintained and shabby. Whatever changes and developments are going on elsewhere in the town do not penetrate to the blighted area, which increasingly lags behind.

Typical areas of this kind have once had, but now lost, an active source of local employment. They are to be found near docks and harbours which have lost much of their trade, round factories which have become obsolete and closed down, also round old commercial centres which have been superseded by newer and more attractive centres elsewhere in the town. There are two attractions in devising improvement schemes for areas of this kind. The first is simply that they are depressing and almost certainly unhealthy. They may well be centres of crime, partly because they are centres for the unemployed and the down-and-out. The second attraction is of quite a different nature. Because blighted areas tend to be depressed and under-used, they appear to be good subjects for new development, which would give the area a fresh start. Very often this view of their potentialities is strengthened by their nearness to active and growing areas requiring the kind of expansion discussed a few pages back. There appears to be every prospect of transfusing vigorous life from the healthy area to the ailing one and so contributing to the health of the whole community.

Difficulties of Improving Blighted Areas

The rehabilitation of blighted areas is certainly important and can be successful. Very often, however, improvement schemes of this kind fail to live up to the full expectations of their authors. Why is this?

The fundamental reason is perhaps that blighted areas never arise without a cause. They are blighted because they suffer from some handicap, some form of inefficiency; the mere recognition that they should be improved is not enough to remove it. Perhaps the commonest handicap is the existence of numerous old and depressing buildings, but it should be recognised that this is combined with the absence of demand for new buildings, otherwise the area would not be blighted but would be developing spontaneously in some new way. Rehabilitation therefore has two parts. In the first place, the immediate physical signs of blight must be removed, and this usually involves a good deal of expensive demolition. Secondly, either the area must be developed in such a way as to give it an entirely new attraction, an attraction which will be reflected in a commercial demand for sites and buildings, *or* it must be redeveloped in a way which will be socially useful, but not commercially advantageous. The first alternative is very difficult to achieve. Whatever the faults of commercial developers may be, they usually know where commercial opportunities exist. The planning authority, in these circumstances, is trying to make a commercial success where the commercial community has not seen the chance of one, to attract activity when this is busily engaged in moving elsewhere. Now the planning authority may be able to contribute some new element to the situation which will transform the commercial outlook, a new road or a new bridge perhaps. It is really the possibility of doing this which makes urban renewal so attractive. Realism involves recognising, however, that in a great many cases this is either not possible at all or possible over only part of the area. Thus, to make urban renewal pay in purely commercial terms is relatively difficult. It is also wise to recognise that we do not fully understand the factors which cause "blight" so that, at present, a certain solution for any single area of blight may well be beyond us.

Naturally this does not exclude the possibility of urban renewal which produces very great social benefits. An old area of decaying property may be cleared, laid out in an entirely new manner and redeveloped with buildings which improve the lives of many people. But the necessary demolition etc. tends to be expensive and the scheme is a financial liability to the public purse. Now it is easy to show in theory that the financial liability is well worthwhile and produces indirectly a valuable dividend for the community. Nevertheless, the imperfections of our economic and social organisations are such that it is extremely difficult to provide without strain for operations of this kind, particularly in poor communities. What makes the situation more difficult is that these expensive, if valuable, schemes usually have to compete with other schemes which are equally valuable, but less expensive. Just as private firms often fail to demolish their old and obsolete buildings because they can move to a new site and start afresh, so public authorities often leave urban renewal aside because it is easier to build urgently needed new houses on bare land at the edge of the town. There is no easy way out of this dilemma. Its ultimate solution must depend upon improvements of our social and economic machinery, but we shall never secure the necessary improvements unless the problem is squarely faced, and that means recognising that a great deal of urgent urban renewal is never going to pay for itself in the simpler sense.

In this connection it is perhaps useful to stress the need for continuous town planning activity. In the past many of our urban problems have been deliberately tackled in a onesided manner in order to deal with accumulated problems. After both world wars, for example, Britain deliberately concentrated at first on the production of more houses, rather than on urban renewal, because doing so was judged to be the means of most rapidly relieving the situation. It now needs to be recognised, however, that every town should put its planning on a permanent basis; this involves recognising that provision for external growth and for internal renewal *must* both be pursued at once. Unfortunately, it is not easy to present clearly the kind of balance that is required.

One advantage of putting our town planning work on a continuous basis ought to be better appreciation of the time element, which has been seriously neglected in the past. We are now beginning to realise that most of our cities, whether we like it or not, are in the grip of a long-term expansion. That should help us to see the inevitability of internal change through growth and to be rather more successful in dealing with its effects. In addition, we should gradually come to have a more intelligent attitude to the replacement of our obsolete and worn-out buildings, a problem that has been tackled very haphazardly in the past.

Many of the towns of today are, of course, far too poor and at present in far too much disorder to develop at once the long-sighted policies which are desirable. Nevertheless, they must work towards policies of this kind if they are ever to emerge from their present tangle of difficulties.

The Limits of Legal Measures

From time to time proposals are made for solving urban problems by a variety of changes in land ownership, land taxation, special rules for the amortisation of buildings and so forth. The merits of these schemes form a complex subject, and the practicability of the best schemes varies from country to country according to local traditions and institutions. No attempt will therefore be made to discuss this kind of scheme here, but it is worthwhile stressing that at best they can only help with the financial problem of improvement which is far from being the only one. No special financial institutions can avoid the difficulty of analysing the improvement problem, of devising the most advantageous solution, of convincing all the various parties that that solution should be adopted, and finally of carrying it out. As far as the carrying out is concerned, it needs to be recognised that help with the financial problem will not help with the actual dislocation inseparable from the actual process of improvement, nor will it solve such problems as the provision of labour and competent contractors.

XI

THE QUESTION OF DENSITY

Density, that is the number of dwellings and consequently the number of inhabitants per unit of residential area, is at bottom a purely practical question. If any intelligent provision is to be made for the growing areas of a town some standard must be set for the number of people in an area, otherwise the public services cannot be economically designed. The water supply system will either be unnecessarily expensive or insufficient for the demand. The sewers will be needlessly costly or overcharged. The roads will be congested or a burden to maintain. Similar problems naturally arise in the commercial and office areas as well as in the residential zones, but the latter tend to dominate the argument because they occupy such a large proportion of the total town area.

Nevertheless, even if density is at bottom a purely practical question, it also has many other aspects, including some highly emotional ones, since it has a considerable effect on people's immediate surroundings and thus on the way in which they live. The history of the discussion of density has therefore been a fairly passionate one, in which the purely practical issues have been coloured by views about different types of environment. This was not in principle a bad thing, but it has led to some overstating of merits and demerits and the practical aspects have sometimes been obscured. It is not the intention of this book to advocate any single doctrine about density, or to suggest specimen figures for density, but the present chapter will seek to show how far various practical considerations must be taken into account in working out *any* solution. It will also attempt to suggest the right approach to the problem of a way of life which is at the bottom of the more emotional parts of the controversy.

Past Attitudes to Density

The various discussions that have taken place on density are too complex to recount in detail, but the nature of the issues can be illustrated by referring to a few episodes.

In those countries that were industrialised in the 19th century residential densities tended at first to be rather high, largely because of the transport problem which was dominated by various fairly rigid systems of railway and tramway. Many of the poorer urban areas erected in this period were congested, ugly and inconvenient, so that in some countries there grew up a serious reaction against high densities.

This reaction found a talented prophet in the Englishman, Ebenezer Howard, whose concept of "the garden city" became important between 1890 and 1900. One characteristic of the garden city as he conceived it was a comparatively low residential density: "twelve houses to the acre". In Great Britain, the advocacy of low density was for sometime an axiom of all urban reform, so that after the First World War, the standard of twelve houses to the acre became dominant, particularly for all "social housing". As it happened, in this same period developments in urban transport, both the invention of the motor bus and that of railway electrification, were making it easier for cities to spread out. It is thus difficult to know how far the change was due to a change in people's ideas of what they wanted and how far it resulted from the fact that a different way of life became practicable.

The same factors which made "twelve to the acre" practicable also made it much easier for wealthy people to live well outside the town in which they worked and to occupy large plots of land where they could have extensive private gardens. In England between 1930 and 1940, four houses to the acre was widely regarded as the standard for a really "good", i.e. well-to-do, neighbourhood, where the standard of housing and amenity was high. "Four to the acre" was never a general development, but these wealthy estates of large, thinly-spaced houses became fairly popular and can be found in many countries, e.g. in the middle class areas of towns like Pretoria in South Africa, in the wealthier suburbs of American cities and in some of the bigger and wealthier towns in countries such as Turkey and Afghanistan. Quite often these well-to-do areas are referred to with pride as if they were representative of the standard of the towns in which they are situated, though in fact the poorer parts of the same towns may contrast with them very sharply and are a much better test of the welfare of the local community.

But this trend to low densities was far from universal, particularly in countries which had a much stronger tradition of apartment dwelling than existed in Great Britain. Densities in many countries, therefore, remained considerably higher, though the change in ideas which had led to the conception of the garden city was widely reflected in a much more intimate relationship between the buildings and vegetation. The garden setting of buildings and the use of trees in streets were developed into a finer art than ever before. In cities like Stockholm the landscape setting of very large numbers of buildings reached a remarkable standard.

Meanwhile in Britain itself a reaction had set in as the result of two different influences. In the first place, much of the "twelve to the acre" development had been extremely badly designed, so that in some people's eyes the whole system came to be regarded as an artistic botch, a form of pretence in which people who were really living in a town tried to pretend that they were living in the country and thus achieved an environment that was an unsatisfactory mixture of the two. Much of this criticism went too far and tended to blame the badness of the conception for the badness of the execution, but on the other hand, the impassioned advocates of "twelve to the acre" had certainly claimed too much for it.

The other influence in Britain was anxiety at the continual growth of urban population combined with the rapid absorption of land resulting from higher standards of space per head, with the result that the sheer physical extent of cities was becoming frightening and led to fears that the rural areas would largely disappear. This fear naturally became particularly acute in countries like England and Holland where the overall population of the country was particularly dense and cities that had once been separate gradually grew together into a single vast urban mass.

Reactions since 1945

As affairs have developed since 1945, the growth of cities has become so obviously one of the major activities of mankind that density has become more and more important, as a sheer question of economy of land. Even in India, where 89% of the population was still rural in 1961 and which has 500,000 villages, several towns already run to millions of people and show no sign of ceasing to grow. In India as a whole there are only about 0.12 acres (about 0.05 hectares) of land per head of the 1961 population, even taking into account all the land that is desert or barren mountain.

In consequence it is tending to become an axiom among town planners that residential densities must be increased and that waste of land is one of the most serious sins of man. There is a great deal to be said for this, but nevertheless the principle can be applied too rigidly and it is worth considering how far it is generally valid.

How Important is Economy of Land?

In the first place it needs to be recognised that evolution of dwellings must depend a good deal on local traditions and circumstances, on local social habits and climatic conditions, for instance. In countries with long severe winters like Canada and Russia, the requirements are different from those in countries where a large proportion of the year can readily be spent out-of-doors. Among other things, this kind of factor is a serious trap when making international comparisons of housing statistics. No-one could say that Turkish housing statistics reflect good housing conditions, but if one knows how much use many Turkish families make of roofs and outside spaces that cannot be classified as rooms, one realises that the statistics of rooms are by themselves somewhat misleading. Every town planner should therefore adjust his views to the conditions of the area in which he is working and should avoid feeling that at all costs he must fall in with some internationally ordained standard. But this is not to say that he can ignore the dangers that have recently caused such alarm.

A very similar consideration applies to the question of economy of land. In certain areas, particularly where the available good housing land is limited by physical conditions (the extreme case is probably the island of Hong Kong), sheer economy of land becomes a dominant consideration to the point of necessitating many practices (such as indoor instead of outdoor play spaces for children) which would be quite wrong in different circumstances. Increase in density may also play a very important part where the dominant problem is not so much the shortage of land as the limited amount of land that can be made available at reasonable cost (reasonable cost including the provision of an efficient system of transport to work).

At the same time, there are still many circumstances in which raising the density is not, and ought not to be, a dominant consideration. One reason for this may be that the organisation of the community in question is not at present geared to the provision of large quantities of high density buildings.

High densities, particularly if they involve blocks of apartment houses and buildings of several storeys, tend to need more elaborate building organisation than the development of the town by separate houses, each within its own small plot. There are other inconveniences to this latter system, but very often its advantages are paramount. The immigrants to many towns are largely villagers accustomed to living in individual houses of one or two storeys. It is to such houses that they naturally turn in the town and the family can sometimes do a great deal themselves either to erect the house or to finish it off and embellish it. On the other hand, if a block of apartments is to be erected, a much more complex financial arrangement will be required. A private individual or a public organisation must invest in the block as a whole and then sell or let the individual apartments to separate occupants. A measure of continuous management of the block is also necessary. In an advanced country with a highly developed society, this is a fairly simple operation which has sometimes been reduced more or less to a routine. In an undeveloped country, the organisation for this kind of operation may simply not exist and, though it would be possible to create it, there may be much more urgent organisational problems to deal with and the limited number of people sufficiently trained to start new organisations may be much more valuable for other purposes.

Are Low Densities Wasteful?

It will be objected that development by separate houses is wasteful of public services and that, as there are so many towns where public services are already in arrears, this consideration should be given great importance. While this general statement is partly true, it has much less force than is generally supposed. In the first place, very few comparisons have ever been made between the cost of developing a large new area with high buildings and the cost of developing it with small houses. To be sound, such a comparison requires, of course, that it should be between small houses laid out economically and the same area laid out with high buildings properly spaced. The comparison tends to be vitiated by pointing out the saving in space that can be secured by substituting high buildings for low without regard to the total space needs of the area. Briefly, the advantage of the high building is that it piles the actual living areas of the families on top of each other instead of laying them out side by side, but it does not enable the same thing to be done with the family's other space requirements, which cannot be provided inside the dwelling. In fact it can even complicate their provision and increase the space they take up owing to the difficulties of providing sufficient means of access to and egress from a building containing a large number of people. Furthermore, buildings of several storeys and particularly buildings of five storeys or more, create complications in the services. Water pressures have to be higher if the supply is to reach the top floor; if the building is high enough, extra pumping may be required which could have been avoided in a low building.

Moreover, a factor that has often been overlooked is that the corridors, lift shafts and access balconies of a big block of apartments are really internal streets and require as much attention to their design as do open air streets. Very often the lighting provided is inadequate and this alone can have a bad effect on the morale of the inhabitants. In addition these "internal streets" can give serious opportunities for crime. America offers a number of examples where this has caused great concern. In general there has so far been too much attention to the mere piling-up of dwelling units and too little to the all-important problem of organising high blocks of apartments as attractive social organisations.

The town planner, then, should carefully refrain from adopting any single doctrine as to the type of building and also as to the density of the new areas that he is laying out and should adjust his methods to the traditions of the society and the circumstances of the town. In small towns the rate of building will be comparatively low; this will increase the advantages of being able to build individual units instead of having to embark on blocks containing several apartments. On the other hand, even in small towns, a certain number of people will probably be anxious to put up flats, and with reasonable ingenuity it should be quite practicable to give reasonable freedom to do both one and the other. What is much more difficult, however, is to give the owner of any individual small plot a right to do exactly as he wishes, since this is tantamount to saying that he can, if he likes, multiply by five or six the need of his small plot for water supply and sewerage. In small towns, too, the problems of distance and the availability of land in suitable quantities are likely to be much easier.

The larger the town, the more likely it is that private or public organisations will exist which are both equipped to build blocks of apartments and willing to do so. In the centres of large and growing towns, moreover, there will be an increasing tendency for some owners of land to wish to replace individual houses by larger and more capacious blocks of apartments. This has its advantages, but can provide the public authorities with serious difficulties, if only on account of the public service problems referred to earlier. This trend therefore needs to be foreseen and a long-term policy adopted. It may not be possible to do this in the early days of a town's growth, when the trends are not yet clear, but one of the advantages of a permanent town planning department should be the capacity to realise that new problems of this kind are arising and to take new measures to prevent them causing avoidable trouble.

Ankara, the capital of Turkey, is a very good example of the problems that result from continued growth. The town is almost entirely a creation of the period since 1920, so that few of its buildings are over 40 years old. Nevertheless, the original buildings in the inner parts of the new town are being rapidly demolished and replaced by others with much larger cubic capacities and containing much larger populations. The impact of this upon the amenities of the area and the increase in the need for public open spaces, and on the capacity of the streets is immediately apparent.

In conclusion, the town planner should perhaps be reminded that we do not yet know a great deal about the best way of living in towns, particularly larger towns, and that we cannot learn all the lessons quickly. Many towns have ancient traditions and habits of life, but towns are now growing so quickly by migration from outside that these traditions are bound to get more and more attenuated. Moreover conditions are changing so rapidly that parts of the old traditions are ceasing to be applicable. The town planner should therefore beware of any theorist who professes to have a cut-and-dried comprehensive answer to the future organisation of towns, particularly if it has originated in a very different country from that where the town planner is working. This need to avoid cut-and-dried solutions makes the town planner's task more difficult, but it also increases the fascination of trying to devise a happy and efficient framework for local life.

XII

TRANSPORT

The motor transport revolution passionately affects us all. We are all either car-owners or anxious to become car-owners, and in either capacity our town life tends to be dominated by traffic, by its noise, by its delays, by the changes and disturbance it causes. Consequently, traffic problems are a subject of perpetual discussion and yet we make little progress in solving them. Elaborate techniques have been devised for analysing traffic flows and traffic regulation of great ingenuity has been introduced and yet, at bottom, we are little nearer to solving the problems.

One trouble is that the motor transport revolution is both so recent and so incomplete. We still have difficulty in understanding its full implications.

And then its effects are so widespread. Many a neighbourhood has found itself transformed by the influx of traffic from other areas, which has disrupted its former peace. Other quiet and settled neighbourhoods are broken up because car ownership changes habits. People develop new needs and move to neighbourhoods better able to satisfy them. Such changes have happened before, but never so quickly or on so large a scale.

We might make more progress with our transport problems if the remedies were not so expensive. Most solutions threaten us with costly rebuilding, but as yet we remain uncertain whether, even if we faced the cost, we should find a satisfactory answer.

Gradually our ideas are changing. The British Buchanan Report on *Traffic in Towns* has made us realise how much we have unconsciously depended on the "general purpose street", which serves as both a throughway and an access and easily becomes unsatisfactory as either. We are now beginning to understand that we need a more sophisticated, more subtly planned, street system, and that this involves radical reorganisation of the areas that the streets serve. To appreciate this need is hard enough. To see its implications and to act on them is far harder. Even where we can glimpse a solution we feel tied down by the problem of resources referred to in Chapter VI. We still do not know how to devote enough of our resources to the needs of communal organisation.

This chapter makes no pretence to solve all these perplexities. It hopes first to point out certain lines of study which must be pursued and certain realities which must be kept in mind if solutions are to be found. Moreover, not all traffic problems are equally complex. In the simpler cases (which means largely in the smaller towns amd in certain new areas), rigorous analysis can lead to a solution which is satisfactory at least for a time.

The core of the problem is, of course, road transport. Even in the heyday of the railways they never displaced road transport as a main means of carriage inside towns and now of course railways play only a limited and specialised role. As far as water transport is concerned, it is possible to point to a few extreme cases, notably Venice, in which water transport has been dominant, but a much commoner role for a town has been that of a junction where land and water transport meet. Today it is possible to say that road transport is the general means of transport *par excellence*, all the others, even where their importance is growing, playing a much more specialised role. For that reason it will be useful to examine the other forms of transport first. That will make the road transport position all the clearer.

Rail Freight Transport

Fifty years ago the rail freight terminals in a town were among the most important foci of traffic, but the fall in rail freight has been heaviest in precisely the miscellaneous traffics which needed to be transferred between rail and road for the end portions of their journeys, and it is in traffics of this kind that continued fall is to be expected. Freight which is carried wholly by rail, for example between mine and smelting works, or between rolling mill and factory, has remained relatively important, but it may not enter the main built area of the town at all and forms no part of the town's ordinary road traffic.

As a result of this decline of rail freight traffic it is often possible to dispense with subsidiary rail freight lines and spurs. This should never be done without considering their possible use for road transport.

Rail Passenger Transport

Fast inter-urban transport by rail may be an important facility where it is available, but it is unlikely to form a high proportion of a town's total traffic. In a small or middle-sized town even the flow of passengers to and from important trains is unlikely to cause any substantial traffic problem.

Rail travel to and from work is only important in a very few towns, and these almost all very big ones. As towns continue to grow bigger the number requiring a purely urban railway passenger system is likely to increase, but the circumstances in which such a system is the best available form of transport improvement and the economics of such railways are still somewhat obscure. Moreover, the merits of each case are likely to depend a good deal on the local geography.

Passenger rail travel can only be successful if large numbers of passengers can be attracted to fairly widely-spaced stations. Where rail travel is in question, therefore, the siting of stations in relation to other points of concourse is a most important matter.

Monorails have recently attracted attention, largely on the ground that they reduce the difficulties inherent in the provision of new urban railways, particularly that of securing the necessary right-of-way in a built area. From a town-planner's point of view, however, monorails are far more like railways than they are different from them. In particular, they resemble railways in their dependence on being able to collect large numbers of passengers at widely-spaced stations, in being comparatively inflexible once established, and in their dependence upon highly developed signalling systems.

An innovation which may prove much more important for the future is the bus which, for part or the whole of its journey, uses a separate right of way, from which other types of road vehicle are excluded in the same way that they are excluded from a railway track. A system of this kind is more flexible than a railway, partly because smaller units can be employed, but particularly because, at the outer, or suburban, ends of the routes the buses can be transferred without difficulty to ordinary roads, making it easier to serve many different settlements and to provide supplementary services as conditions change. The success of any such system, however, remains dependent upon persuading a large number of people to use public transport along a few major routes. Moreover, if the advantages of the system are to be maintained in densely built areas, the provision of the specialised track becomes as expensive as that of a railway, while the movement of really large numbers of people involves, as on a railway, the provision of elaborate signalling and control of headways between vehicles. In certain cases it may be practicable to use the tracks of abandoned urban railways for specialised road services of this kind.

To sum up, passenger rail transport can, in exceptional circumstances, play an important role in the internal working of very big towns. It is even possible, under present-day conditions, for it to be introduced where it has not previously existed. Such cases are, however, exceptional, so that they have little relevance to the general run of town planning problems which form the main theme of this book.

The provision of buses on specially reserved tracks may have a more important future, especially where extensive new areas are being planned as a whole. This, however, is a new technique which has still to be fully worked out.

Water Transport

Whether water transport is by sea, river or canal, it is the terminal or port which constitutes the most important feature from the town planner's point of view. The sea, rivers and canals are, of course, important physical features which may affect the development of the town in various ways, but this influence is quite different from the results of the handling of their traffic.

For practical purposes, ports are of two main types.

(i) *The port for purely local services*, such as the links with off-shore islands. A port of this kind is a focus for traffic rather like a railway station. The ships are unlikely to be large, the services will often be frequent and regular and passenger traffic may be important. This type of port is likely to be in the town or just on its edge.

Although rapid advance in the technique of bridge building is causing many short-distance ferries to be replaced by bridges, the traffic on other longer, but still fairly short, sea-routes is expanding rapidly as a result of the drive-on, drive-off type of ship which carries complete vehicles. These often tend to replace former train ferries, but they are also used on routes such as those to and from Ireland for which train ferries were never developed. It is not at present easy to see where competition will settle down between the "drive-on ship" and the use of containers (referred to below), but the longer drive-on routes only appear to develop where a substantial tourist traffic is in prospect, as with the recently established vehicle ferry between Le Havre in France and Rosslare in southern Ireland.

With the "drive-on" ships truck-trailers are sometimes carried separately, a different towing vehicle being used at each end of the sea journey, so as to save weight. This is a sort of halfway house to the container system which is revolutionising sea transport for many types of general cargo. As containers are removed completely from their wheeled base for shipping, their handling requires special lifting apparatus, and this tends to concentrate container operations in a limited number of ports. At present, however, the container revolution is proceeding so rapidly that it is far from easy to see what its full effects will be. It seems clear, however, that container ships will be loaded and unloaded much more rapidly than the former general cargo ships. Considerable marshalling of vehicles may be necessary in the vicinity of a ship, but on the whole the operations which take place within the dock area are simplified and the amount of dock employment is certainly reduced.

(ii) *The port for long-distance services.* – Some longdistance sea transport is being affected by the container revolution. In other trades the evolution of very large bulk-cargo ships is restricting severely the number of main terminals, though there is some redistribution from these by smaller ships to smaller ports. Here too, the ultimate effects are not yet clear, but one effect is that it is becoming increasingly difficult to see the future of a port except when it is examined from the national point of view.

A modern long-distance port is likely to stand outside a town rather than in it, as an old-fashioned harbour used to do. In this it rather resembles a very large modern industrial plant such as a petroleum refinery or a steelworks. Such very large plants are often closely associated with a port, and the resulting industrial aggregation becomes a major influence on the whole development of the neighbourhood.

Air Transport

Even if a town benefits from the use of an airport, the latter may be so far away as to have no material influence on the town's planning problems. Where an airport is as much as 20 miles away, however, its sheer extent may have a significant effect on communications for miles around, particularly as a consequence of aircraft noise, which at present must be admitted to be an unsolved problem. Moreover, where really big town growth is concerned, the existence of an airport may have an important influence on the directions in which it is possible for the town to grow.

Even today, the total road traffic to and from an airport rarely becomes a major factor in the whole town traffic. Nevertheless, it may play an important part in planning on account of the importance of ensuring that the transit to and from the airport is easy and rapid.

The Crux of the Modern Transport Problem

Reverting now to road transport, which is the central problem, it is worthwhile first of all to take a closer look at the circumstances in which the typical modern transport problem arises. It is essentially due to three main difficulties:

(1) the enormous increase in the number of vehicles wishing to use streets whose physical capacity cannot easily be adjusted;

(2) the additional difficulty caused by parking, i.e. the occupation of street space by waiting vehicles, many of them idle for long periods;

(3) the special difficulty of enabling dense streams of traffic to flow

smoothly at junctions where many individual vehicles wish to cross the path of others.

In addition, it may be emphasised once more that the difficulties are made much worse by the rapidity with which conditions change as the number of vehicles increases and new traffic movements develop.

All the above problems can be solved where two conditions are fulfilled:

(a) where there is plenty of space;
(b) where there is plenty of money.

Granted the fulfilment of these two conditions, it is possible to construct the elaborate split-level road junctions which first became a common feature in America. In the existing built areas of towns, however, neither the space nor the money are available, the expenditure being enormously increased by the existence of buildings which must be demolished in large numbers if radical improvements are to be made.

It follows that the traffic problem is rarely serious in secondary and minor streets, though there are important exceptions.

In particular, where a new area is being laid out, an experienced town planner who is able to make use of effective control powers should be able to ensure that the local street system is both safe and convenient and that it will remain adequate indefinitely, provided that the original land uses are not radically modified. The limit on the effectiveness of the planning of such new areas arises where the new local street system feeds into major arteries affected by the traffic problems of other and more difficult districts.

As far as old areas are concerned, many districts laid out before the dominance of the motor vehicle are spacious enough to cope with any expansion of their own traffic, provided again that the land uses are not altered. Some of these older districts, however, are apt to be invaded by streams of traffic from areas of quite a different character, especially commercial and industrial centres. This is partly a result of vehicles seeking routes alternative to the congested main thoroughfares and partly because certain cross routes which used to be quite insignificant now carry large numbers of vehicles.

Ancient Towns

In the most ancient parts of towns, both in old Asian cities and in the medieval towns of Europe, the streets may be so narrow and winding that they are wholly unsuitable for more than very small volumes of traffic, and even, as in the old parts of Antakya in south Turkey, unusable by wheeled vehicles at all. Sometimes a reasonable solution can be found by maintaining such old districts as purely pedestrian areas. This was recently the situation in the old part of Antakya and is partly the position in a town like Siena, where a large proportion of the vehicles park outside the old city. A solution of this type is usually only practicable, however, because the newer parts of the town are of quite a different character.

Patrick Geddes demonstrated in India at the beginning of this century that modern streets could sometimes be cut through such areas without destroying their original character if this operation was conducted with sufficient care by what he called "conservative surgery". This is not always possible, however, and the district may need to be reconstructed for other reasons, particularly if the buildings need to be replaced by more satisfactory and more stable structures. The future of the area then ceases to be primarily a transport problem and becomes a matter of sympathetic neighbourhood design.

The Crux is to Manage Heavy Traffic Flows

Despite the local importance of these special problems the crux of the modern urban transport problem consists in the management of heavy traffic flows. The analysis of such flows is therefore one of the main preliminary tasks.

The Objectives of Traffic Analysis

It happens all too often that serious study of transport problems begins only as a consequence of the appearance of traffic congestion and the desire to find a remedy for it. As a result, investigation of traffic problems is dominated by a narrow concern to relieve congestion in a particular street. It will be seen below that this is both a legitimate exercise and one that can sometimes be pursued in isolation. It is, however, of great importance that the problem should also be looked at more broadly. In this, as in so many other aspects of town planning, a sound study involves approach from more than one angle, followed by a consideration of how different factors interact.

For the present, then, it can be accepted that study must include observation and analysis of traffic streams, which are usually very complex, their composition varying, moreover, according to both the hour of the day and the day of the week.

To study such complex traffic streams would be hard enough if they were stable, but in the present period they rarely are, partly because the town is usually growing and partly because the motor transport revolution tends to increase movement faster than the population grows. Whatever the present state of affairs, therefore, one can assume that movement will increase. Accordingly, present traffic conditions have only a limited importance; what is most needed is information about the future. This can be considered at various levels and from various points of view, as the following paragraphs will show.

(i) *Immediate Detailed Traffic Control.* – Many towns have not yet derived full benefit from modern techniques of traffic control, so that the flow of traffic through the existing streets can sometimes be improved by skilled detailed regulation. Improvements of this kind may well be worthwhile, even if they only afford relief for five years or so, and in considering such short-term schemes it is of course the changes over the next few years which matter. These may be relatively easy to foresee.

(ii) *Simple Redevelopment.* – In addition, it may be possible to secure a material easing of traffic flow by a comparatively simple street improvement. Such improvements are sometimes fairly inexpensive if they fit in with the rebuilding plans of individual developers, and some are of permanent value even if much about the town's future is obscure. The removal of "pinch points" in old streets is probably the simplest example.

(iii) *Major Change.* – But the serious problems involve much more fundamental work. In the first place, traffic changes often reflect the type of fundamental change in the town which is discussed in Chapter X, "Internal Improvements". In the second place, an enduring remedy clearly involves looking more than a few years ahead. The forecast must cover a period in which the detail of the expected changes is very difficult to foresee. In ten years, for example, the population of a town may increase by 50%, while the number of vehicles in it may double and new types of industry may settle there, causing new types of transport movement. This kind of major change involves considering the traffic problem more broadly, and here the town planner's main work starts to help. We have seen that the planner concerns himself with how fast the town will grow, in which directions its growth should be directed and how the activities in it will change. These are the main factors which will determine the future trends of traffic.

Study of traffic problems therefore needs to be closely linked with the general study of the changes taking place and to be expected in the town. If activities in the town alter, the resultant traffic will alter too, but the reverse does not necessarily hold. Even if activities remain the same, the traffic arising from them may alter, as when an industry adopts a new form of transport, perhaps using more road transport and less rail. Moreover, although the size of a residential population may remain much the same, the traffic it generates may increase greatly, simply as a result of people acquiring more cars.

The following are points which it is important to investigate:

External Traffic

(i) How much traffic enters the town from outside and how much of it comes from a distance as compared with that which originates in the town's sphere of influence?

(ii) Is a significant proportion of the external traffic anxious simply to pass through the town on its way elsewhere?

(iii) Is there any significant amount of *daily* travel to work in the town from nearby communities?

Internal Traffic

(iv) What are the main travel-to-work movements inside the town?

(v) What are the main generators of traffic inside the town? and what is the nature of the traffic they cause?

Public Transport

(vi) What part does public transport play?

Forms of Transport

(vii) Is one form of transport tending to replace another, e.g. more use of road and less of rail?

All the above questions should be studied as far as possible in terms of trends. It may not always be possible to ascertain the trends, but this must be one of the most important aims. It will be easier to see what is happening if all these questions are examined for the light they throw on the working of the town. For example, if a bus undertaking is showing a declining revenue, this should not only be examined to find out in which part of the operations the loss is occurring, but should also be compared with changes in the town which may be responsible.

Scientific traffic analysis involves the use of elaborate and sophisticated techniques, for which it is best to employ a specialist. A thorough-going traffic study is, however, a lengthy and expensive business, which should only be undertaken after very thorough planning. If cooperation with the specialist is to be really successful, those seeking his services should have thought very carefully about the problems, and in particular about the changes in activity which are causing the changes in traffic. These might be described as the "non-traffic elements" in the traffic problem. It is also important to be clear as to how far possible solutions of the traffic problem must be conditioned by policy decisions made on other grounds. Sometimes, for example, it is important to reserve a very large flat site for some use for which it is particularly suited. If that is the aim it will be important that it should not be cut up by new roads.

Summarising the Significant Points in the Traffic Situation

Before consideration is given to the employment of a traffic specialist, the most significant factors affecting the traffic problem should therefore be picked out, even if the full extent of their influence cannot be gauged.

A beginning should be made by considering foreseeable transport changes outside the town, as these may materially influence the local situation. At Adana in Turkey, for example, a new road through the Taurus Mountains will for the first time introduce an important traffic stream into the town from the North-west. In Afghanistan, the fine new road from Kandahar to Herat has greatly diminished the importance of the ancient town of Farah, which no longer stands on an important through route.

Once the main outer communications have been studied, the internal situation should be examined primarily in terms of centres which create or attract traffic and the nature of the flows associated with them. This broad examination may lead to very difficult conclusions. It may emphasise some major difficulty such as the need for extensive redevelopment of the town centre, for which no solution is in sight. It is very important to recognise the difficulties at this stage, even if no solution is available, or even if some problems cannot be fully understood without lengthy further study. A problem must not be ignored because it cannot at present be solved. Even if temporary and only partially satisfactory measures have to be adopted, their value can only be judged in the light of the problem as a whole.

Where traffic difficulties exist, it is possible in principle either to shift the source of the traffic or to improve the routes along which it flows. In practice, however, it is rarely possible to shift a source of activity primarily in order to relieve congestion. Where this does prove possible it will probably be part of a general replanning of an area due to a number of causes, a subject which is further discussed in Chapter X "Internal Improvements".

On the other hand, non-transport reasons may involve considerable shifts in the centres generating traffic. This may be necessary because technical changes in industry require factories to use a new type of site or in order to open-up new residential areas so as to reduce overcrowding in the older parts of the town. Transport facilities have to be adjusted to changes of use more often than the other way round.

It is customary to lay emphasis on the desirability of separating the different types of traffic, particularly with the object of improving traffic flow by excluding the slowest units, such as horse or ox-drawn vehicles. This principle, however, needs to be applied with due discretion, particularly as it is often far from easy to enforce. In minor streets, intended primarily to serve as access to buildings, all forms of traffic must naturally be admitted. If some forms of traffic are to be banned from major streets, either an alternative route must be provided for the banned vehicles or the effect will be to prohibit the use of such vehicles entirely over large areas of the town. The latter course may be justified, but it is a serious step to take, particularly in countries where animal transport is still important, and the issue should be faced directly. Prohibition should not be an accidental by-product of what was intended merely as a restriction.

If it is proposed to split up a traffic stream, care must be taken to understand its composition thoroughly. Failure to do this has often led to errors. There have been important misconceptions as to the proportions of certain traffic which wished to bypass the town and as to the predominant turning movements in the town centre, so that considerable study has been given to systems of relief roads which later proved to be mistaken remedies.

Reorganisation of traffic streams must be accompanied by effective control of land use, or the revised road system may be largely stultified by the spontaneous growth of new land uses. A striking example of this is the failure of the British planning system to control frontage development on bypasses built between the two World Wars, with the consequence that the through traffic capacity of these important highways was seriously reduced. Likewise, a bypass that had been intended to lie permanently outside the town was sometimes made less useful by the more or less unplanned development of land beyond it, so that an unforeseen flow of traffic across the bypass came into existence.

It is important that reorganisation of traffic streams should take into account the needs of all the users. Otherwise the new traffic arrangements will certainly be evaded, to the detriment of their efficiency. In particular, if vehicular traffic is compelled to follow longer and more circuitous routes than hitherto, it cannot be expected that pedestrians will do the same. Unless convenient paths are provided for the latter it will be impossible to stop them trespassing.

The most dramatic recent transport innovation is perhaps the multilevel road junction. For a very large city in a highly developed country such junctions are evidently of increasing importance, but, as already noted, they have two serious disadvantages. They are costly and they require a great deal of space. Because such junctions are impressive there is a danger that their inherent difficulties will be overlooked. In fact, a tendency has already appeared to over-prescribe them for poor cities in developing countries, where the money should be spent upon something else, probably improved housing. Improvement of housing and of transport offer in some ways an interesting contrast. Improved housing affects primarily the individual in his private capacity and, though it contributes to efficiency as well as to happiness, its social effects are not readily *visible.* There is a consequent tendency to underrate them. Improved transport has the maximum visible effect and this causes many people to overrate its contribution to welfare.

Parking

Serious study of traffic problems is bound to involve the problem of parking, the crux of which is the tendency to use road space for the storage of vehicles for long periods. Short calls by vehicles cause much less serious problems, though they can be awkward by reducing the effective number of traffic lanes in narrow streets with heavy traffic flows. In some communities the biggest single difficulty is the individual who drives to work by car in the morning and leaves it occupying roadspace all day. Long-period parking can easily result in a situation in which it is virtually impracticable to use a car for short calls or to carry out necessary loading or unloading during ordinary working hours in quite a large area of a town.

The remedy must lie in some form of restriction of parking on the carriageway, usually a total prohibition at some points combined with a time limit at others, enforced by means of parking meters or otherwise. It is important, however, to recognise the conditions of a successful parking control policy. Car-owners form a constantly growing body, so that any restrictive policy must be clearly shown to be both necessary and constructive. Regulation of parking must therefore be defended on the ground that it is, on balance, an improvement of the situation. This normally means that it must be accompanied by some improvement of off-street parking facilities.

Secondly, the administrative work of parking control is bound to be heavy and expensive. This means that there must be properly trained enforcement staff and also, what is equally important, a control authority which has a strong and consistent policy and knows how to gain the support of public opinion.

Once the motor vehicle has become a permanent feature of a town's traffic, regulation of parking is bound to be a permanent need; otherwise the temptation to obstruct the roadway with one's car is bound to be irresistible. By degrees, however, the problem should change in that off-street parking facilities (not necessarily free) should become more and more frequent, with the consequence that, in certain areas, parking space will become an important land use.

In very heavily motorised areas the conflict between need of space for cars and other purposes remains partly unresolved. This is one of the great contentions about how to organise the modern town. It will be evident from the above, however, that car parking must not be regarded as a separate "traffic" phenomenon. It is also one of the main land use problems.

Public Passenger Transport

One of the inescapable, and still unresolved, effects of the motor transport revolution is its influence on public passenger services. Any substantial modern town has been accustomed to depend on a fairly highly developed public transport system, usually served by buses. As the number of private passenger cars increases, fewer people use public transport services, whose finances consequently deteriorate. This leads to some cutting of services, as a result of which the carless members of the community suffer and controversy sharpens. It is not possible to say that controversy begins at this point, because there has always been an undercurrent of argument as to how far the convenience of the public, rather than profitability, should be the dominant consideration in organising the services. Even where a decision is taken to subsidise the transport services as a whole, this does not avoid argument; the principle of subsidisation does not settle how far it should be pushed in the direction of maintaining highly unprofitable services. Moreover, as motorisation increases, the revenue of the public services is apt to go on declining for a depressingly long time.

The increasing numbers of private cars usually have the effect of slowing down traffic generally, including the public transport services, with the consequence that these services become even less attractive. In the larger towns, the point may be reached where the growing difficulty of parking cars in the town centre drives a proportion of car users back to public transport, a move that may be accentuated by the introduction of systematic parking controls. These normally have the effect of discouraging long period parking, especially daily travel to work by car, in favour of short period parking for business or shopping purposes.

These movements, however, are subsidiary to the main trend and do not alter the general problem, of which the main features are the following.

(1) Less favourable results from public transport, combined with a continued need for it.

(2) A general worsening of traffic conditions on the main routes, which has the effect of worsening the public transport services.

(3) Up to the present, a continued increase in motor vehicles, even where car ownership is already high, so that pressure on available thoroughfares (and also on parking facilities and controls) continues to build up. We can make certain deductions about future car ownership levels, but in many respects it is still difficult to see what the effects will be on people's habits, including the extent to which even car-owners will prove to have a residuary use for public transport services.

The future of public passenger transport in towns must be regarded as another unsolved problem. Many experiments are being tried, and many of them have made possible partial improvement in conditions, but no really satisfactory answer of wide application has yet been found in the more difficult cases, partly because, as noted above, private car ownership is still increasing. Certain points are, however, becoming clear.

(a) When, as a consequence of an increase in private cars, public transport services cease to pay their way, they should not be lightly abandoned. Their importance may increase again as increased congestion causes difficulties for individual motorists.

(b) The management of public transport services should recognise that a rapidly changing and highly competitive situation lies ahead, in which the public transport services should be overhauled and improved to increase their attractiveness. The financial arrangements for public transport should therefore allow of a certain amount of new investment, despite the deteriorating financial outlook. In the long run it will be more economical not to let the transport equipment become semi-derelict before it is renewed.

(c) When methods of alleviating traffic difficulties are studied, the needs and importance of the public transport services should always be borne in mind. In particular, where substantial central redevelopment is being planned, the opportunity should be taken, if possible, to create improved conditions for public transport.

(d) Whether the present level of private car ownership be high or low, an increase in car ownership should be regarded as one of the most important developments to be expected sooner or later.

Categories of Street

Western cities have traditionally been based on the "all-purpose street". That means that, broadly speaking, any street communicated with any other street and was open to traffic of all kinds. The street was normally lined with buildings on both sides, which had direct access to it. This kind of street has become less and less suitable with the growth of fast-moving vehicular traffic and in central areas it has already been widely modified in one respect: by the imposition of one-way traffic rules which greatly ease the flow of vehicles at the cost of some lengthening of journeys.

Recently opinion has swung increasingly against the all-purpose street, though naturally it continues for the present to be the predominant type except in a few recently developed or redeveloped areas. A good deal of controversy continues as to the best street system for a large town with a high ratio of vehicles to population, but certain basic principles have become well established.

(a) The purpose of each street should be clearly decided and its planning should reflect its purpose. The smallest streets should simply enable the occupants of the adjoining buildings to move into the traffic circulation system. As far as possible they should not be through-traffic streets, so that they are not encumbered with vehicles that have no business in the immediate neighbourhood.

The next grade of street should provide the main circulation within limited areas and also the necessary access to the main streets designed for lengthy journeys. The planning of these second-grade streets should ensure that the junctions on the main through streets are kept to a minimum. These second-grade streets will naturally be of larger capacity, but will not be planned primarily for fast movement. Neighbourhood shopping centres etc. should be close to such streets, but not actually on them, so that the shoppers etc. are well-separated from the traffic stream. As few buildings as possible should have access directly on to such streets.

The main streets should be planned primarily for fast, safe movement of large volumes of traffic, with a minimum number of carefully designed junctions. No buildings should have direct access to them. They should give ready access to, but should not pass through, the main centre of the town.

(b) As far as possible, pedestrians should be able to circulate freely on separate pedestrian paths so that they are not endangered by vehicles. In particular, they should not have access to the main streets referred to in the immediately preceding paragraph.

These principles are unexceptionable, but they need to be applied with due discretion, particularly in areas where the population is as yet unaccustomed to elaborate traffic regulation. Many countries have successfully introduced one-way streets, because offences against the one-way rules are easily detected and, once the one-way system is working, offenders are a patent nuisance to all other road users. Some other forms of road regulation are much more difficult to enforce and enforcement should not be attempted unless it is evidently both practicable and worthwhile. Much will obviously depend upon the efficiency of the control of land use and the arrangements to limit the access to buildings from certain streets. Elaborate rules about pedestrians also need to be avoided. It is a sound general rule that no pedestrian will readily take an inconvenient course, such as not walking across a main road where and when he wants to, unless actual physical barriers prevent him doing so. In certain countries pedestrian discipline has been brought to a high level by intensive police work, but this is difficult to do and should not be attempted lightly.

Street layout will always depend largely upon the way the land between the streets is used. The main land uses should therefore be determined before the streets are designed. Technical highway considerations may then require some modification of the original land use proposals, but the opposite system of beginning with the roads is bound to lead to confusion.

Summary of the Present Outlook on Transport

The reader may feel that this chapter has been unduly negative, but where a problem is, in fact, largely unsolved, it is important that this fact should be frankly faced. We can only see town planning problems squarely if we recognise that we do not know all the answers. Moreover, we need to distinguish clearly which answers we do not know and to concentrate on those.

At the same time, it would be a mistake to regard our transport perplexities as a purely technical transport matter. They go far beyond that for they raise the question of what we want to do with our new inventions. How far are we prepared to sacrifice other things to the pleasures of mobility, or can mobility be bought at too high a price in damage to our environment? It is not enough to answer these questions in general. To say that "we should design for the free use of the motor car" gets us nowhere. The fact that we live closely packed in cities means that we need not a general solution, but a highly practical specific solution to which we can adjust our physical equipment; a solution, moreover, which can be applied by degrees as we gradually replace our inherited buildings.

XIII

TECHNICAL ASPECTS OF TOWN PLANNING

As has been emphasised earlier, town planning means arranging for the good management of the town. Whatever the town's present condition, a sound future for it involves providing certain public services which can only be organised communally. They must be provided for in all new areas to which the town extends; in existing areas they must either be installed if they are lacking, or adjusted as conditions change and the demand for services changes with them.

The principal services concerned are roads, sewerage and drainage, water supply, electricity and the collection of refuse or garbage. In some towns there may be other services such as gas supply or the provision of public transport, but the presence or absence of these makes no essential difference to the fundamental problems presented by the group of services listed above.

Each of the above services:

(i) is influenced to a greater or lesser extent by the topography of the area;
(ii) is affected by the requirements of its own technique;
(iii) costs money and
(iv) is difficult and expensive to alter once the main physical apparatus has been installed.

Four important results follow from this. First, the way in which the town is laid out must be influenced to some extent by the physical and technical requirements of these services. Second, the technical solution adopted must be influenced by the amount of money available. Third, because the installations once made are difficult to alter, considerable foresight must be shown in planning them. Fourth, the lay members of the town planning authority need to have a general understanding of the technical problems of public services, if they are to deal efficiently with the problem of providing money for them.

How Does Topography Affect Services?

One of the first matters to which a town planner should direct his attention, therefore, is how the physical characteristics of the town will affect the design of services and how he can best provide a satisfactory system of services with the money that can be expected to be available. This is one of the most important reasons why a town planner should both know the town's topography, and know it in depth. For what matters is not simply the shape of the ground, but also the nature of the soil and sub-soil. Sloping ground formed of strata that naturally hold the water may present more difficult drainage problems than flat land with good porous subsoil and a low water-table. Two areas of flat land which look alike to the layman may be very different to the planner because one provides good foundations for buildings and a low water table, while the other has a high water table which makes both building and drainage difficult. A town planner with years of experience will think of many of these things more or less subconsciously; he should remember that what is so clear to him may not be so clear to others who need to understand them if they are to follow his conclusions.

Drainage

In town planning it is never easy to give a distinct priority to any one point. It is essentially an art in which a number of matters have to be thought about together. Nevertheless there are reasons why a town planner should think first of all about drainage, because that is the service in which he must be guided to the maximum extent by the natural shape of the land. Electricity, unlike water, has no difficulty in "flowing" uphill, and the comparatively small quantities of water required for domestic purposes can, if necessary, be pumped uphill much more easily than the large and irregular volumes of water that must be dealt with in drainage.

The ideal urban drainage system is one which successfully disposes of all storm water and at the same time conveys all wastes from buildings to a treatment works, the effluent from which is sufficiently pure to be turned into a river without causing pollution. (There are limited variants of this such as the purification of sewage in sea water, but the technical points need not be pursued here, as they make no difference to the general principle.) Such a system of comprehensive drainage and sewerage is so much the most satisfactory available, partly because it is the system easiest to run without breakdowns dangerous to health, that it has at present no rival where it is practicable. Every town planner will therefore regard it as an ideal and will be wise to shape his plan with such a system as the final aim, even if it cannot be installed at once.

Comprehensive drainage and sewerage are, however, expensive to construct and need skilled design, which is not yet available everywhere. Moreover, they present the peculiar difficulty that, once constructed, they are almost entirely out of sight, so that people are much less conscious of the benefit of good drains than they are of a good water supply which enables them to drink from a tap whenever they feel like it. Moreover, sewage is unpleasant evil-smelling stuff and therefore not a popular subject. Finally, although it is comparatively easy to make a water supply pay for itself out of the charges to consumers, this has usually been found more difficult with sewerage, which thus tends to appear as an awkward debit item in the municipal accounts.

For all these reasons, the number of cities without comprehensive drainage and sewerage is extremely large, and there is no prospect of this state of affairs being remedied quickly. Nevertheless, comprehensive sewerage and drainage are a most urgent need of modern towns, and one has an entirely false view of town planning unless one understands what an important role this very humdrum service is bound to play in it.

Realism involves recognising, however, that there may have to be a transitional period in which some town life has got to be organised without sewers, and there are various partially effective substitutes, such as the regular collection of night-soil. The great thing is that the thinking about all these matters should be clear-headed. If a second-rate substitute has to be used for the present, this should be recognised and the future aim, for example the construction of sewers by stages, should be definitely settled.

By far the commonest substitute for sewerage is some form of subsoil absorption, but usually this is not a system. It simply reflects the state of affairs that has grown up through gradual expansion of the town without thought for the future. There is no doubt that in many conditions a large amount of sewage, including human faeces, urine and other putrescible wastes, is "successfully" absorbed into the subsoil by means of seepage from cesspits, garbage pits, etc. The word "successfully" here means that the material is gradually broken up so that ultimately it becomes harmless. There are certain cases where the word "successfully" need not be put in quotation marks, because the community is small, the ground water level low, the subsoil porous and the subsoil water not used for human consumption. Where these conditions exist, one must be thankful for them; they may represent the best solution for the immediate future.

Usually, however, there is a price to pay, and the commonest price is pollution of the ground water. A less common trouble, which becomes increasingly frequent as towns grow, is the emergence of pools of sewage on the ground surface in lower parts of the area, as a result of the increased volumes of liquid soaking into the earth. Temporary flood pools may do no harm if the flood water is not contaminated, but where the subsoil water is impregnated with sewage, the flood pools will be polluted too and can be a serious source of nuisance.

In many areas shallow wells are used for domestic water supply, including drinking, and the pollution of these shallow wells through the seepage of sewage into the subsoil is a frequent cause of disease. The obvious remedy for this state of affairs is the provision of a pure supply of piped water, but this presents certain problems where the subsoil is polluted. It is broadly true that even the most efficient water supply systems are not leak-proof, and many systems have a great many leaks. Moreover, in many towns the water supply is still intermittent, so that the mains are often empty and it is then comparatively easy for polluted subsoil water to enter the water supply system.

The provision of a public water supply always has the effect of increasing the consumption of water per head of population, and this also increases the volume of sewage. For this reason, it has been recognised that water supply and sewerage should always be planned together, but this ideal is rarely attained. Moreover, the resulting evils must be expected to increase rapidly if the present state of affairs is allowed to continue. Towns are increasing and water consumption per head is increasing too, both of which cause a rise in the volume of sewage. Thirdly, a situation that appears tolerable for a period of years may conceal a real deterioration through the gradual accumulation of sewage in the subsoil, so that polluted pools eventually begin to form at the surface. The technical problems of sewerage are well understood, so that problems are soluble once the determination is there to solve them. The first requirement is that they should be given a sufficiently high priority. This book does not attempt to deal with the technical problems, which are adequately treated elsewhere. Its aim is to make clear how they must be fitted into the overall thinking.

Before leaving the question of sewers and drains it may be observed that they need not follow the lines of public roads; but if they are not to do so, they must be separately provided for in the planning of the area and there must be sufficient access to them.

Water Supply

It has already been remarked that the planning of public water supply is easier than planning drainage and sewerage because water for a public supply can be more easily pumped uphill. Indeed the layout of a water scheme often includes a means of raising the main supply to a convenient height which will ensure sufficient pressure in the distribution network. Nevertheless, largely on account of the problem of pressure, the whole water supply network must be planned as a consistent whole. As a matter of technical convenience it is usually divided into sections, but the sections must be properly related and the technical details must be clear in advance. Here again, therefore, foresight is necessary for efficiency. It should be noted, too, that the necessary foresight involves deciding what areas are going to be developed and also the density of the future population. Otherwise the necessary volume of water supply cannot be calculated, and the water mains will not be of the correct size.

The fact that development always takes place gradually emphasises the need for close cooperation with an experienced water engineer. If a sewer draining by gravity is constructed at once to a size which will only be necessary after a considerable lapse of time, it will work quite efficiently even with a small flow. With water mains, however, the factor of pressure raises more complex problems when the main is large but only a small supply of water is required.

Electricity

Electricity, the other main service to be expected in every modern town, is much less dependent upon contours, since electricity has no difficulty in travelling uphill. It too, however, is dependent upon comprehensive planning if the equipment is to supply the necessary loads without wasteful expenditure. Consequently, the forecasting of areas and loads is fundamental in this case too. The supply of electricity is unlikely, however, to be a deciding factor between two possible layouts of the town.

Roads

Roads are the last general service to be considered here. They are less dependent upon contours than drainage or water supply, but on the whole they are the most complex service of all from the point of view of design. They are the most costly of the services, and have peculiar features such as their tendency to be blocked by stationary traffic. There is no equivalent to parked cars in a sewer or a water main. Moreover, roads are the only one of the services here discussed in which the traffic is visible and audible to those living on adjoining land, and in which the inhabitants themselves take part in the traffic. Roads can thus be a serious source of both discomfort and danger. However serious the problems resulting from increasing needs for water and drainage, the problems of increasing road traffic are at least equally great, while the solutions have been less completely worked out. There is also a far more radical difference between a main road and a minor residential road than between a main water pipe or sewer and a small branch distribution pipe. Modern engineering techniques enable roads to be built with very high traffic capacities, but the problem of junctions between heavy flows of traffic is still partly unresolved. Dramatic results can be achieved with multi-level road junctions in open country, but the junction problem which concerns the town planner is that which creates the innumerable links between the main traffic arteries and the dense buildings of town centres. The complexity of the movements makes the required pattern very complex and the density of the buildings makes change very expensive.

For these reasons the problem of roads has been subdivided in this book as follows:

(i) main routes are dealt with in Chapter XII "Transport";
(ii) minor roads are discussed in connection with the layout of neighbourhoods (see below pp. 139-41);
(iii) certain problems of change are referred to in Chapter X on "Internal Improvements".

In many countries road traffic is still at a low level, and European or American road authorities would laugh at what some towns regard as "congestion". If there is any prophecy that can be made with confidence, however, it is that the near future will see an enormous and widespread increase in road traffic. The future volume of a town's traffic therefore needs to be the subject of most careful thought (see Chapter XII "Transport").

Naturally, care and efficiency in the planning of services are not enough to make a good town plan. In particular, they are not enough by themselves to create a pleasant environment. It needs to be repeated, however, that efficient design of services is an essential *basis* for the amenities which every town planner wishes to provide.

Detail Planning

It is one of the inescapable difficulties of all urban planning – and also of all urban building – that the occupation of the land is very dense, so that virtually the whole of it is used in one way or another. The only areas not used are either unusable (precipitous slopes, for example) or bits of derelict land affected by blight or, perhaps, small areas which, as a result of bad planning, have been left without access.

The town planner is not himself concerned with all the details. Even under the most stringent town planning regulation a great deal of detail must be settled by the occupant of the land. Nevertheless, for reasons which have been set out earlier (see Chapter XI "Density"), the town planner must be concerned with some detail if he is to carry out his task of organising communal services and protecting the individuals in the town from being a nuisance to each other. This control of detail can be exercised in several ways, the choice depending partly on local traditions and conditions.

The possible methods are broadly as follows.

(a) The map of the town can itself show a good deal of detail; for example, the precise boundaries of the plots to be used for various purposes, the building lines, the exact future road boundaries etc. This can be done by preparing first a master plan for the whole area and then adding detailed plans, as required, for the areas where development is imminent.

(b) Detail can be settled little by little as applications are made for the approval of new buildings.

(c) General rules can be laid down on certain matters such as minimum distances between buildings, access to buildings, provision of loading facilitities which do not encroach on the main road, etc. This method always has to be used to some extent, because some forms of regulation cannot be shown on a map. The purely town planning regulations of this type necessarily shade off into regulations concerned with health, fire precautions and structural safety.

The present development of town planning as a flexible form of control is to some extent a reaction from the fact that written rules and regulations were found inadequate, largely because they could not be sufficiently adapted to local physical variations.

The first of the above three methods has the advantage of providing maximum advance certainty; it is therefore particularly valuable where there is a shortage of trained men for the administration of town planning control, who can negotiate flexibly and responsibly with those wishing to erect new buildings. Conversely, this method is rigid and particularly disadvantageous where the optimum layout cannot be easily worked out in advance. In fact, it is difficult to apply it fully except in residential areas to be developed with single-family dwelling-houses. Where blocks of apartments are to be erected, it is difficult to determine the size and shape of the blocks satisfactorily in advance. With industrial buildings the difficulty is even greater.

The second method is the most adaptable, and in many ways the best, but there should be no illusions about the difficulty of working it satisfactorily. It requires subordinate staff able to deal flexibly and responsibly with applications for development, and the public must regard them as trustworthy. The official handling each application must have thought out the problems of the neighbourhood a good deal already, but without letting himself become rigidly attached to one detailed solution. A balance must be struck between giving advance guidance on essentials and leaving details to be settled day-by-day.

The third method, as already noted, always has to be used to some extent, but it has its own disadvantages. In the first place it is difficult to draft regulations which are legally sound and at the same time clear and easily understood. Moreover, there is the inevitable dilemma that what is clear and simple to administer may easily become rigid and unsuitable for a rapidly changing world. When drafting general rules there is also a standing temptation to give too much weight to idealism, with the result that the prescribed standards become impracticably high, so that well-meant regulations become dead letters.

Accordingly, none of the three methods is very easy to use and the whole subject may seem to lead to a frustrating tangle of bureaucratic rules, too confusing to be used effectively. This, however, is too gloomy a view. Good management and the use of a mixture of methods to suit the circumstances can result in clarity and ease of working, but only if the whole administrative issue is given the attention that it needs. Once urban living becomes a dominant feature of human affairs, as is now inevitable, the machinery for organising the physical details of towns must have a prominent place in our lives and should be administered by first class officials, since it is one of the most difficult problems of the day. Really good town planning administration is still comparatively rare, but there is sufficient evidence of what can be achieved to show that a great deal is possible. Likewise, really good and intelligent developers are still rare, but the best of their kind show that they can make an important contribution to good town development.

Amenity

In this connection it will be as well to say a further word about the "amenity" aspect of planning, which must be considered in detail. The word "amenity" is here used deliberately instead of some such word as "aesthetic" because the latter is too narrow to cover everything concerned. Quietness and convenience are amenities which the town planner should try to promote, but they would not be covered by the word "aesthetic".

The ultimate object of town planning is to make a town pleasant to live in, just as the ultimate object of an architect is to make a house pleasant to live in. But just as a house cannot be pleasant unless it is both structurally sound and also useful, so a town cannot be pleasant unless it is also efficient in a variety of ways. In a sense, therefore, the whole question of amenity, or pleasantness, must be a secondary rather than a primary one. This is not to diminish in any way its importance, but simply to stress an important condition for creating amenity. Much town planning criticism would be more valuable if more care were taken to distinguish comments on the efficiency of a town plan (how far it provides necessary services economically and so forth) from comments on its amenity aspects. It is possible for a plan to be efficient but uninspired.

It also needs to be recognised that the achievement of amenity is not wholly under the planner's control, save in a few new towns where the planner may be able to dictate almost every detail of the environment. Normally, the planner must allow individuals a good deal of freedom to create the details of their environment in a way which appeals to them, even if he considers that that way is mistaken. Many of the most criticised forms of British building between the two world wars were due to inexplicable accidents of taste, such as the widespread fondness for "half-timbering" even when it only amounted to a form of applied external decoration.

Even to the extent that amenity is under the town planner's control it is very difficult to write about it in a book of this kind. It raises many problems of design which can only be discussed at considerable length and are therefore best dealt with in a separate volume. Moreover, even a town planner who is a master of design may be in a dilemma in judging how local habits and ways of living are going to develop.

Local Habits

Local habits result from a blend of climatic influences, social customs and economic circumstances, all of which are likely to change in the 20 years ahead. It might perhaps be expected that climate would remain a more or less constant factor, but specific adjustments to climate often reflect the resources that were available at the time and may change with the advent of other resources, such as different and cheaper fuels, availability of refrigeration, etc.

The influence of resources is particularly important in the matter of the type of building that is economically practicable. At present the world is full of communities where the housing situation is so bad that the most urgent need is whatever form of new housing will do most to improve quickly the conditions of a large number of people, even if the result is something below the optimum standard of amenity. If progress continues, therefore, we shall be faced with a difficult process of upgrading a great deal of housing.

The most serious problem, however, must be to know how local living habits are going to evolve, insofar as these depend upon inclination and social custom. In some communities the long-standing tradition of strict privacy for womenfolk has broken up so much that it must be expected to diminish its grip also in other communities which at present retain it. Yet a change of this kind is difficult to count on when planning for the future. The same kind of problem arises with the "extended family".

Where it still exists, it must be expected to break up, to some extent at least, yet this cannot be taken as a general rule.

For these reasons, every planner must find his own solution to the problem of planning for amenity in the light of local circumstances and his own genius. This book will confine itself to indicating certain factors which he must consider and the limitations which they impose.

Even when one has recognised to the full the need to leave many points to the individual developer, there are certain matters of detail which planning control must deal with. No attempt will be made here to set out standards for this detailed control, but it is important to understand what it should cover, and why.

In this matter of detail it is not easy to distinguish between the requirements of good layout, of safe construction, and of other considerations such as the prevention of fire. In order to discuss the reasons why control is needed, however, it is not necessary to distinguish all these overlaps. They are important mainly for deciding the precise standards to be imposed.

The following are the main points to be considered.

Use Zoning

In general, the town planning movement of the 20th century has aimed at separating the main types of use, collecting factories in industrial zones, shops and offices in commercial zones, and so forth. Recently this system has been attacked as pedantic and unnecessary, partly because industries are now less smoky and noisy than they used to be, so that there is much less case for keeping them apart from other kinds of building. How far is this recent attack on use zoning justified?

The short answer is that use zoning, like any other form of control, has sometimes been applied rigidly and unimaginatively but that there are sound practical reasons behind it, such as the following.

Industry. – (a) Certain industries either cause objectionable fumes or need to be very carefully regulated if they are not to do so. This latter group, even if harmless most of the time, is always liable to be a nuisance to its neighbours if the normal method of regulation breaks down for a short while. These industries, which are few in number, need to be very carefully sited, preferably at some distance from other buildings and, where there is a prevailing wind, down wind from the town. Examples are steelworks, cement works and several types of chemical industry.

(b) All industries are liable to cause noise from the running of machines, from loading and unloading etc. Even if a building is at present occupied by a more or less noiseless industrial process, the process may alter or a different manufacturer may move into the building. On the whole, therefore, new industries are best established in separate industrial zones. On the other hand, where an existing factory is already established among houses, there may be no urgent reason to move it.

(c) Even small factories normally require larger sites than many other types of urban building. Moreover, they need, if possible, to have space on to which they can extend at short notice. Their requirements for electricity, gas, water and drainage are often on a much larger scale than would be required by residential or commercial buildings of a comparable size and they often cause much traffic, both for the carriage of goods and for the assembly and dispersal of personnel. This traffic may have to continue during the night. All these points make it much easier to meet the need of industrialists and to avoid nuisance to the non-industrial elements of the population by grouping factories in specially equipped industrial zones. Some of these zones can be quite small and they can be sited in several different parts of the town. (See Chapter XIV, "The Planning Process", pp. 137-38, for other comments on the siting of industrial buildings.)

Shops and Offices. – (a) Such buildings are centres to which customers come from a distance, even if not from the remoter parts of the town. They should therefore be placed where they are easily accessible from all the areas they are intended to serve, and should be so arranged that they can deal with large numbers of people and associated traffic. These considerations make it natural to group such buildings at nodal points, an arrangement which has the additional advantage that a customer can visit several of them on a single journey. This general principle should not be interpreted too strictly. One or two isolated shops can sometimes be advantageous. There is ample evidence, however, that such shops, when ill-placed, have been unsuccessful and the ruin of a series of shopkeepers.

(b) Some kinds of office can be established in a dwelling without causing disturbance and exceptions can reasonably be made for these. They are mainly the type of office with a staff of only one or two people and very few customers who call at the office. On the whole, however, offices as well as shops require specialised sites. If they are interspersed with dwellings they are either inefficient or else they disturb the amenity of the latter.

Space about Buildings

If buildings are allowed to be indiscriminately contiguous the results are (i) dangerous, (ii) unhealthy, (iii) disagreeable, and (iv) a cause of congested traffic. On the other hand, the owner of each individual site has a natural tendency to feel that the necessary space should be provided by his neighbour rather than by him, and the builders of small dwellings are often too ignorant to realise what bad conditions they are in danger of creating. The planning authority must therefore lay down minimum rules about (a) setback (if required) from the street, (b) loading and unloading facilities within the building's curtilage or compound, (c) distance of the building from other buildings and from the boundary of its plot. (This last may, of course, permit a degree of contiguity with other buildings, such as continuous development of the street frontage.) The distances prescribed under these various heads will depend upon a mixture of considerations: fire prevention, ventilation and fire-fighting, for example.

Height of Buildings

This is important for a variety of reasons:

(i) it affects density, the number of people frequenting the building and the volume of traffic associated with the building;
(ii) it affects the lighting of other buildings;
(iii) it affects the details of the structure required for safety from collapse;
(iv) it affects the fire-fighting problem.

As stated above, no attempt will be made here to discuss the detailed standards to be imposed for all these various purposes. The standards must depend on many local factors, such as climate, the type of construction to be used in each building, local habits etc. The main point is that every regulation should have a specific purpose, which each official concerned understands and can explain convincingly to members of the public.

Similarly, no attempt will be made to discuss the complex question of control of structure from the point of view of safety, freedom from damp, adequate ventilation, adequate circulation space etc. It will be evident, however, that these matters are best dealt with along with those discussed above and not made the subject of a separate control.

These detailed regulations will apply either to all buildings or to buildings of certain classes, for example, to all houses or all shops. They should therefore be drafted very clearly and made freely available to members of the public, to ensure that everyone preparing a plan for a new building takes them fully into account. Needless to say, it is useless to prescribe such standards unless all plans for new buildings are examined in order to see that they comply with the standards, and the buildings are inspected in the course of erection in order to see that the approved plans are being observed.

XIV

THE PLANNING PROCESS

Previous chapters have reviewed the main problems with which a town planner deals and have sought to explain how he should analyse them. This has left largely untouched the question of how to draw conclusions from his studies and to decide what needs to be done. It will be evident, of course, that his conclusions about different problems need to be related. They must not be mutually contradictory or lead to unforeseen complexities. That is implied in the making of a plan.

This further stage, the main planning work, is a many-sided activity of which it is difficult to give a coherent picture. The present chapter will therefore concentrate on describing what is involved in the more important spheres and will leave to a further chapter the process of pulling together all the various conclusions into a single programme.

The Main Operations

The essence of the planning work lies in the following operations.

(a) Extension of the Town:
   (i) deciding how much additional land is needed;
   (ii) selecting the actual areas to be used;
   (iii) allocating them to the various different uses;
   (iv) working out the detailed organisation necessary to enable them to be used.

(b) Improvement of the Town:
   (i) deciding what changes in the existing body of the town will be required by the trends within it and also by its growth;
   (ii) working out detailed schemes of improvement;
   (iii) arranging these in a programme to fit in with each other and with the extensions of the town.

In practice, the work is more complex than this list would suggest. This is primarily because a town is a living thing with large numbers of independent organisations at work within it.

Previous chapters have made clear that the planner must take full account of what is already happening and of the strength of the forces at work. Even when the spontaneous developments are favourable, he must thoroughly understand them in order to provide the services that they require and to ensure that the necessary developments do not get into each other's way simply because they are separate and have not been planned as a whole.

An Essential Dualism

Often, moreover, the spontaneous developments are not wholly favourable; the planner must then judge how far communal action should and can be recommended to correct their defects. He must make the most of spontaneous developments and yet he cannot be entirely passive. In order to understand the essence of this stage of the work it is essential to insist on this dual aspect.

This dualism applies to all the processes of growth and change. They cannot be completely resisted and yet they must be resisted enough to guide them to some extent. A particular difficulty is that we have very little control over the tendency for changes to occur simultaneously when we should much prefer them not to, or over the tendency for them to occur in an unwelcome order. The planner's practical proposals and his programme for carrying them out must in part be dictated by the trend of events, and yet he must avoid being wholly dominated by the trend. In explaining his proposals to others, he must constantly be alert to explain what forces are at work and how far they can be controlled.

A first problem is, of course, the order in which the town planner can best tackle the solution of the problems. It is impossible to be definite about this, but there is a certain logical interdependence of the different issues which entails making certain decisions before others; failure to observe this logical order is one of the most frequent causes of mental confusion in planning. A particularly common error is perhaps to start on the reorganisation of road traffic without considering first of all what activities are creating the traffic and how they are themselves liable to change.

Town planning must include extensive detailed work, because so many physical installations have to be fitted so closely together, but this detailed work cannot be well done unless the broad relationships have first been understood. The present chapter will therefore concentrate on the broad analysis.

Problems of Expansion

The work deriving from the expansion of the town divides itself naturally into the following stages.

(i) Broad selection of the areas to be developed in the light of several different criteria: proximity to the existing town, adaptability for particular purposes, physical suitability (ease of drainage etc.), present and future transport facilities etc.
(ii) Sub-division of each area to be developed according to the type of use and the size of unit required. The important subdivisions are:
  (a) industrial areas;
  (b) public buildings requiring large sites, including universities and colleges;
  (c) residential neighbourhoods and associated school sites;
  (d) shopping centres;
  (e) amenity areas;
  (f) the transport network.

The present chapter will not discuss these subdivisions exhaustively, but will bring out some of the important points.

Industrial Areas

Once the planner has some idea of how many people will require industrial employment in the future it is natural that he should start to consider where the industrial areas are to be. At once he encounters an interesting example of the perpetual dualism of his work, for two quite different factors may determine the siting of industrial areas: (i) the need to reserve for industry land which is specially suitable for that purpose (sites with special transport facilities or the large flat sites required by certain processes such as steel-making), and (ii) the desirability of providing industrial employment within reasonable reach of residential districts, especially if the latter are extending rapidly into new areas where no employment exists. These two factors may or may not suggest different answers. Everything depends upon the terrain and the industries involved. In general, only a few industries have stringent siting requirements, but some of these are so exacting that such industries are not always sited in or adjacent to existing towns, becoming the focus of specially created settlements. Petroleum refineries are perhaps the commonest examples of this, while steelworks are another.

Where these stringent requirements are not in question, the situation may be said to be more or less the opposite. That is to say that the industrialist will often be less concerned with the physical peculiarities of the site (provided that it is reasonably level) than with the facilities that he can obtain there, including the labour supply. A wide range of industries will therefore be willing to settle in several different parts of a town, provided that certain conditions can be fulfilled. These may be summarised as follows:

(i) a reasonably level site of appropriate extent, obtainable on reasonable terms;
(ii) certain standard public services, especially electric power, water and drainage: power and water need not always be supplied on an exceptionally large scale, but they must be reliable; drainage may not need to deal with exceptionally large volumes of sewage, but may nevertheless be one of the most important determinants of the siting;
(iii) good transport and communications for three purposes; receipt and despatch of materials and finished goods; travel by the labour force to and from work; management and commercial negotiation.

Accordingly, only detailed examination of local circumstances can show how far it will be necessary for the housing areas to be determined by the industrial requirements, or the industrial areas to be influenced by the situation of the most suitable housing areas.

Industrial areas are likely to present most difficulty where there is very little level land. In such cases the need to place the industries on the few physically suitable sites may be a powerful determining factor in the plan.

Administrative Buildings

From many points of view, public administration should be considered along with industry because it is often a major element in employment. Many administrative buildings (such as the main blocks of a provincial administration) need to be grouped together so that they constitute as large a focus of employment as a substantial factory.

The question where administrative centres should be placed in a town plan does not admit of a simple answer. Some administrative offices have to be frequented by numerous members of the public seeking to secure permits, to pay taxes etc. They should therefore be on central sites and, in certain instances, divided into sub-offices serving different districts. Other offices (public works planning, purchasing, educational organisation, higher law courts) need to be in fairly large groups and some (such as the main public works offices) need not be central.

Higher Education

A university or large technical college is rather a special case. The number of people concerned (perhaps over 10,000) and the space required are both very large. Consequently, it is more or less out of the question that the university or college should be on a central site, though there is much to be said for it being in a striking and attractive position.

Many a town planner, desperately trying to secure control over development that is uncurbed, may feel that an analysis of the above type so much simplifies the situation that it bears no relation to reality. In particular, where there has been no town planning control hitherto, industrialists sometimes appear to behave more or less irrationally, being in fact concerned to secure a suitable site or some facility such as rail or port access before it is snatched from them by a competitor. This is a very real difficulty in many areas, but if planning is to stop this kind of confused scrambling and substitute something more rational, the fundamental requirements must be well understood. Special local and administrative measures may be required in order to bring the situation under control, but they will only be successful if they can be shown to meet real basic needs.

Residential Neighbourhoods

The word "neighbourhood" is used here to emphasise that when land suitable for housing purposes has been found it needs to be organised into appropriate units. The idea of a "neighbourhood" has been the subject of a good deal of controversy, but here it simply represents the fact that residential areas need to be organised round centres for certain services. Schools and shops are the most important, with schools perhaps the most influential of the two.

The first requirement is naturally to find land which is conveniently situated in relation to the town, but it must also fulfil certain other criteria, the foremost of which is that it must be conveniently drainable. (See Chapter XIII also, "Technical Aspects of Planning".) Secondly, the land must be conveniently related to the places where people work, some of which are likely to be far from the town centre. Thirdly, the land must be capable of being organised into convenient school units. This involves roads from two points of view. First, there must be convenient roads and paths to enable children to collect at the various schools (primary and secondary schools may be in different places). Secondly, it is important that children going to and from school should not have to cross major thoroughfares unless they can do so safely and conveniently by means of a bridge or an underpass. This means that small areas of land cut off by a main road may be unsuitable for residential use.

There are, of course, optimum sizes for schools and maximum distances which children can be expected to walk to school. These two factors determine the approximate area which should have easy access to a single primary school and are probably a more powerful influence on the layout than is the need for conveniently sited shops.

Schools are thus a primary factor in the whole design of residential areas. Naturally it is not possible to predetermine closely the number of children of school age in a given number of families at any one time. Nevertheless a good deal of waste is avoided if the distribution of school sites is broadly related to the expected school population of the surrounding area and if easy access to the schools is a factor in the design of the local road system.

In addition, of course, the residential areas should be laid out so as to be attractive to live in. But there is no question of "either..or". If the residential areas are not convenient this cannot be compensated for by providing amenities of other kinds.

The local provision of shopping areas is always necessary to some extent, but the number of shops required in a neighbourhood varies with local custom, with the size and character of the town concerned and with the distance of the neighbourhood from main shopping centres. Local shopping in a new neighbourhood generally builds up gradually, and it is easy to underestimate the demand in the light of what happens in the first few years.

Excessive claims have sometimes been made for organisation in neighbourhoods. It is doubtful whether, as has sometimes been claimed, the layout can make a serious contribution to fostering social intercourse between new residents who did not know each other before they came to live in the same new area. But even if excessive claims have to be discounted, the neighbourhood idea still has considerable practical usefulness for the above reasons. It may be useful to enlarge somewhat further on its influence on the local road pattern. The design of a neighbourhood's roads should meet the following requirements.

(a) It should provide satisfactory links between the neighbourhood and other parts of the town. This involves junctions with main roads, which should be limited in number and carefully designed.

(b) It should provide satisfactory communication with the focal points within the neighbourhood itself, especially the schools and shopping centres and places of public resort.

(c) Its design should contribute to the safety of road traffic.

(d) It should be economical in road cost.

At the same time, it must be remembered that a new residential area always develops gradually, sometimes quite slowly. At any one moment, therefore, the partially developed area should not look like an unfinished mess. Some untidiness in a partially developed area is unavoidable, but it can be minimised with care.

All the above objects are more easily pursued if the new residential areas are divided into neighbourhoods, partially self-contained, but also articulated with one another and with other areas of the town.

Amenity Areas

A town's amenity and recreation areas will to some extent be conditioned by local topography. Many an old town has long-established places of public resort which should be protected; in new towns there is usually a beach, a riverside, a hill or some other natural feature which should clearly be reserved for recreation even if it has advantages for other purposes.

As a general rule, however, the recreational areas of a substantial town cannot be limited to natural features of this kind. A major requirement is the provision of numerous neighbourhood open spaces, and in most countries these should normally include games fields. Areas of this kind should be designed after the selection and arrangement of the residential neighbourhoods, but in selecting the latter the need for interspersed recreational areas should be kept in mind. The whole question of the size and design of recreational areas is a complex matter, as yet far from fully developed and dependent very much on local habits. A new development such as television can so change family habits that outdoor recreation needs change too. In the next 20 years the proportion of the urban population which has been urban for a considerable time will increase greatly and it is to be hoped that its standards of life will rise. As a result, its demands for means of recreation are likely to increase and to change, but it is not easy to see what the changes will be.

Improvements

So far the discussion in this chapter has been confined to the results of expansion of the town but, as has been seen in Chapter IX "Growth and Change in Towns", expansion in itself causes dislocation; in any event, changes independent of expansion are continually causing dislocation too. The planner has to provide for both of these, but the improvement problem will not become clear to him until he has roughed out his general plan for extension. Once he has broadly mapped his new areas, he will see how they affect the balance between the various parts of the existing town. This in turn will throw light on the effects of other disturbing trends.

One or two examples will help to make clear the kind of broad problem that becomes evident in this way.

Adana, Turkey. – In this ancient town the commercial centre was orginally south of the east-west road which is the town's most important communication link. When the town started to grow rapidly, it appeared that the best situation for many of the new residential areas would be to the north of the town rather than to the south. If the town plan adopted this as the basis for expansion it would involve the question whether the old commercial centre should be extended or displaced northwards and this, in its turn, would affect the kind of scheme prepared for the relief of congestion in the old centre.

Swansea, South Wales. – This town is on the coast, so that the directions of extension are limited. For many years growth was predominantly westwards. Most of the new housing was in that area and a big new industrial estate was also sited there. Meanwhile, the old industries on the east side of the town were decaying, leaving a large derelict area remarkably close to the town centre, which did much to cut off the eastern housing areas from the main body of the town. It became evident that the whole future shape of the town would depend on what was done with this decayed area.

Sheffield, England. – This town developed in a valley in the Pennine Hills and became one of the most important centres in the world for the manufacture of high quality steels. By the time of the Second World War, the lower part of the valley was built solid with a mixture of small houses, small workshops making hand tools and large factories making specialised steels and products manufactured from them. There was a severe shortage of houses and many of the existing houses were subject to a disagreeable amount of dirt and noise. The factories, besides being much too close to the houses, had great difficulty in expanding and reorganising because the adjoining land was built up. It was clearly necessary to build many houses outside the original valley, but this meant fusion with neighbouring towns and the danger of damage to an important landscape area which had been made into a National Park. Many of the factories needed to be moved to new sites, but this was expensive and technically difficult and the relations between individual factories were extremely close. The siting of the necessary new developments therefore presented very complex problems. Improvement and extension of the town were inextricably involved with each other.

Preparation of a Plan

We can thus begin to see the kind of working-out process that goes on in the planner's mind, as a result of which, starting from a "map" of the existing town, he gradually develops a "plan" of the town of the future. It is worth discussing for a moment the distinction here made between "maps" and "plans". These words are often used loosely and more or less interchangeably, but the former can be considered as a means of showing the existing situation and the latter as a means of presenting ideas for the future.

The preparation of good maps is a more difficult task than is commonly realised, because every map involves a careful selection from the material which, in theory, could be shown upon it. Few users of maps pause to reflect how much information has been ingeniously suppressed in order that they may see clearly the points which one particular map is intended to show. "Motoring maps" and street maps are two common types which, as a moment's thought will indicate, deliberately give only a limited amount of information about the areas they cover. Even the familiar "physical" maps which we have all studied in school geography classes suppress a great deal of detail unless they are on a very large scale. Maps that try to show all the available mappable information about an area are in fact extremely rare. Almost every map is a specialised product for a particular purpose, and a town planner must create the specialised maps that his work requires.

As he studies the evidence about the town, the planner will decide which parts of it can usefully be presented in map form and how various maps can be combined to show useful combinations of information. This is an important first step. Although maps that try to show too much are apt to be simply confusing, composite maps providing simplified information can be very valuable provided, and the proviso is important, that they are accompanied by sufficient written information. It is of the greatest importance to realise that maps cannot show every aspect of the situation. Like statistical tables they usually need to be combined with a written argument.

The maps which a town planner uses are, of course, those that illustrate the planning problems. Maps of natural drainage areas are clearly of great importance in deciding how the town should be laid out. Very often the important features can be reduced, for the specific purpose in view, to quite simple indications. This helps to turn the map into a basis for a plan.

A map is useful for the conclusions which can be drawn from it, but it does not itself furnish those conclusions. A plan, on the other hand, is a series of proposals for the future and always consists to some extent of conclusions drawn from a map. It may also need to embody some map material to make itself clear. But it is important to realise that a plan cannot be prepared until a design problem has been defined. Nothing can be designed or planned "in the air". The designer must have been given instructions, even if he has given them to himself. Thus a plan is always a product of a train of thought, even a plan containing a large element of aesthetic design.

This gives a further illustration of the dual character of the planning process which was referred to at the beginning of the chapter. The further a planner gets into detail, the more he will be concerned with questions of design rather than with purely practical considerations. The general shape of his road layout will be determined by questions of topography and access, but the details of the roads will include a certain aesthetic element. It is important that the planner should be aware of this transition from the practical to the aesthetic and should understand the claims of each. Otherwise he will muddle his eventual justification of his proposals.

The Technical Aspects of Drawing Plans

No attempt will be made to deal fully with this here, but its importance should be stressed. Every town planner will have to develop his own detailed method, dependent partly upon the nature of the maps readily available to him and partly on his resources. The problem is

(i) to show clearly the existing situation and at the same time the changes proposed for the future;

(ii) to bring out a variety of points about the future without making the plan confusing. It is necessary to show which areas are to be used for different purposes and sometimes the order in which they are to be used. Some boundaries need to be precise and rigid. Others need not be.

In all countries, including developed ones, there is the difficulty that, ideally, the plans should be examined and understood by a large number of people, whereas many people find it difficult to understand plans. Sometimes an attempt is made to meet this difficulty by preparing extremely simple sketch plans, illustrating the points in a diagrammatic form. This solution needs to be used with care for the following reasons. First, the planner needs a carefully drawn and accurate plan both for his own purposes and for demonstrating the essential points to the town planning authority. Having worked out a suitable technique for this purpose he should standardise it as much as he can, so that people get accustomed to the symbols he uses. Secondly, it is arguable that sketch plans are more suitable for the expert than they are for the layman, since the latter finds their highly simplified form of expression even more remote from reality than the fully detailed plan.

Certain problems cannot really be simplified and to attempt to do so is to evade the issue. This perhaps applies to the problem of getting laymen to understand plans. It is perhaps better to train them by constant explanation of carefully drawn plans than to prepare sketches which offer new opportunities for misunderstanding.

Emergence of the Crucial Difficulties

In this process of working out detailed proposals, the planner will naturally start from the easiest points. He will pick out quickly the decisions for which the evidence is fully adequate and which can be made without prejudicing other issues. Sometimes very large areas of the plan can be satisfactorily outlined in this way.

Even where the evidence justifies only tentative conclusions, this will not necessarily cause serious difficulty. For example, if the area required for future industry is uncertain, it may be possible to provide for a contingent extension of the industrial zone on to open land without displacing other buildings and without absorbing land of first agricultural quality. One reason why the planning of large towns is so difficult is that so many of the sites allocated in the plan are bound to be closely surrounded by other built areas, so that there is no room for the kind of latitude referred to above.

Having dealt with the easier points, the planner will gradually distinguish certain questions which are both difficult to answer in themselves and also the keys to other decisions. The difficulty is the greater when one operation, such as bridge-building, must necessarily precede another, the development of the areas beyond the bridge, for example.

Gradually, therefore, the planner will arrive at a list of outstanding issues, which will fall broadly into the following categories.

(i) Matters on which it is difficult to decide *what* decision should be made. (Should the port be developed to take bigger ships; is an additional commercial centre required; should the river be bridged for the first time?)

(ii) Matters in which the question is *how much* to do. (How much provision should be made for the replacement of artisan industry by factories; how much housing should be retained in central areas despite the need for decentralisation; how far should services for new industry be provided in advance?)

(iii) Matters in which the question is *when* to take action. (When to build a major bridge, when to clear and rebuild particular housing areas, when to redevelop a congested centre).

These outstanding issues are the essence of preparing a synthesis, which is discussed in the following chapter.

XV

SYNTHESIS OF AN OVERALL POLICY

The previous chapter examined how a town planner starts to draw conclusions from his studies of the town's development. It is now necessary to see how he arrives at a comprehensive set of recommendations, consistent with each other, and how they should be presented.

To understand this final operation it will be well to start by stressing certain features of a town planner's conclusions which affect both the way he has to think about them and the form in which he presents them to the town planning authority and to a wider public.

(i) His conclusions are based on evidence of varying quality.
(ii) They vary in the degree of certainty attaching to them.
(iii) They vary in their finality.
(iv) They must often represent a compromise between conflicting needs.
(v) They concern action to be taken over a series of years.

At the cost of some repetition it will be worthwhile illustrating these points.

Quality of Evidence. – Deductions from physical facts may be very reliable and final; for example, conclusions as to the load-bearing qualities of certain soils. Many planning conclusions must, however, be based upon evidence which involves a degree of uncertainty, such as forecasts of population growth. The planner must always be careful not to conceal this unavoidable element of uncertainty either from himself or from those he must convince and he should take considerable trouble to explain in simple terms why, despite this uncertainty, his conclusions are both necessary and reasonable.

Certainty. – However reliable the evidence may be, it may not be sufficient to make a firm basis for the necessary conclusion. For example, the evidence of recent births is conclusive as to what the population of school age will be in the near future, but it remains uncertain how far many of these children will proceed with their schooling, especially at secondary school level. Nevertheless, some working conclusion about this latter point must be formed in order to make a sound judgment about the size of the school-building programme.

Finality. – Some conclusions need not be final, others must be. For example, it is important to form a working conclusion about the rate at which the town will grow and to base immediate action on this, but the conclusion can be open to revision in the light of experience and it is sometimes important to recognise the need for such revision. In this connection it is worth noting that overestimation is sometimes less dangerous than under-estimation, provided that the element of uncertainty is recognised. If it is estimated that the population of a town is likely to grow from 50,000 to 75,000 in something between 10 and 20 years, it will for many purposes be easier to work on the faster rate of growth and later to adjust downwards, if necessary, than to adjust upwards when too low an estimate has been made.

As compared with this, certain conclusions need to be final despite all difficulties. If a new river crossing is in question the site should be chosen as soon as possible and the choice should be *adhered to,* for the siting of the crossing will affect the approach roads and the use of the adjacent land for some time before the bridge is built. Likewise, the width of a new road must be settled before it is built, however difficult it is to foresee the volume of traffic that will use it.

Compromise. – It is tempting to think that some considerations, particularly beauty, are so important that they should never be sacrificed. In practice, however, this is not practicable and it is better to recognise this, since if one attempts to shut one's eyes to this problem, one is sooner or later driven to compromise on an unsystematic basis. Compromise, of course, can be done badly but, as in so many other matters, one cannot avoid mistakes by refusing to face the issue at all. The whole question of the expansion of a town may involve encroachment on natural beauty, but there will have to be expansion all the same. Clear thinking will assist rational analysis of the potential losses, of the countervailing gains and of the comparative advantages of different solutions. Dislike of compromise often means that the merits of the issue are not realistically faced.

The Time Element. – This has several aspects.

(a) *Preparatory Work.* – If a school must be ready in a particular year, necessary "action" decisions will have to be taken at least three years earlier. But even earlier work may be necessary to make the school site accessible for the preparatory work. Considerations of this kind may not show on the actual plans, but the necessary action will not be understood unless points of this kind are taken into account.

(b) *Feasibility.* – The form eventually selected for certain developments may partly depend on whether they have to be carried out before or simultaneously with certain others. The programme of works can only be adjusted to a limited extent in accordance with needs. For example, neither the road programme nor the school programme can be expanded more than a certain amount over a short period. A major feature such as a bridge or tunnel may involve postponing certain other activities while it is built.

On the other hand, expenditure which is impracticable now may be perfectly feasible ten years hence, when resources will have expanded along with the growth of the town, and this may be an important factor to emphasise in presenting the programme.

(c) *Decay and Obsolescence.* – It is essential to remember that the stock of buildings in the town is getting steadily older. This is particularly important if there has been intensive building at a date just sufficiently remote to mean that in a few years time the necessary rate of replacement of old buildings will rise sharply.

Nature of the Synthesis

The planner must therefore be thought of as making a large number of coordinated recommendations, the nature of each depending partly upon the situation as a whole and partly upon the particular problem in question. On account of the need to convince many different people with a great variety of interests, the recommendations need to be put forward as a reasoned whole, which shows how they are related causally and also shows the various priorities (economic, social, aesthetic, constructional etc.).

Naturally, a successful presentation of this kind is far from easy to achieve, and this explains why the presentation of town plans has usually been their weakest feature. One difficulty was the belief that the only really important element in town planning was the "plan" itself in the sense of the actual design on paper. Even when it was realised that the plan needed to be supplemented by a written explanation, there was still a tendency to treat the latter as subordinate to the plan, whereas in fact the whole problem is so dynamic that successful presentation involves treating the written exposition as the heart of the matter and all plans, diagrams and statistical tables as illustrations of the written argument.

In particular, the reasons behind the recommendations and the nature of the necessary judgments cannot be stated except in writing, and all complex relationships, particularly relationships in time, need words to make them clear. Finally, it is very difficult to use plans to illustrate any kind of qualification and it will by now be apparent that the conclusions of a planner are bound to be full of qualifications. He may put forward very specific recommendations about the use of land for this or that purpose, but the judgments involved may have to be highly qualified, though this does not reflect on their soundness.

If the presentation is to be as complete as suggested above, the way in which the argument is developed is clearly of the greatest importance. The problems of towns are so varied and, in particular, their immediate needs are so diverse, that the presentation of the problems of each town must vary a good deal too. Nevertheless, certain general lines for a presentation can be laid down. In the outline sketched below it is assumed that the problems of the town are being presented for the first time, so that all the necessary background information must be included. In other words, there can be no reference back to existing informative documents.

Suggested Outline of a Town Planning Report

1. *Physical Background.* – This is a good point with which to begin because the physical background of the town is more or less unchanging (which does not mean that it cannot be changed).

The problems of writing this part of the report are apt to be deceptive. Because this section is a description of natural features it is often thought to be easy to write, whereas in fact little attention has been given to the art of making clear which natural features are important to the question of town development. Natural features which are irrelevant for this purpose should be omitted. There will be quite enough points to consider without dragging in unnecessary ones. A map should illustrate the important physical features, some of which, such as a high water table, may not be readily visible to the layman.

2. *The Existing Town.* – At this stage the description should be of the town rather than its problems. The latter cannot be understood until it is clear in what kind of a community they are occurring.

This section naturally includes a good deal of fairly simple information about population, the chief local activities etc. The difficulty is the qualitative appraisal. There are real and important differences between towns and it is very important to note the peculiar characteristics of the town being studied. Towns, however, are living and changing entities and the process of describing them, which easily leads to their classification into groups, is apt to produce a misleadingly simple impression as a result of concentrating on the leading characteristics only. It is all too easy to emphasise qualities common to several towns and to discount exceptional points. Even if a town can appropriately be described as belonging to a well-defined type, it may also be in some respects an exceptional example of that type, and this may be its most important characteristic.

A map of the existing town should be prepared which brings out as far as possible the critical points, such as the relative densities of population and buildings and the main traffic movements.

3. *The Future of the Town.* – Once the nature of the existing town has been discussed, a good foundation has been laid for considering its future. In the light of what was said in the previous chapter about the dual nature of the planner's work, it will be evident that this section must start from the existing spontaneous internal developments. To these must be added possible influences on the town from outside, such as the deliberate planting of industries there by the national government. Then reference must be made to the physical problems which the expected growth will produce.

Types of Change. – The changes to be considered in the town will be of three main kinds.

(i) Changes that are already taking place, such as the growth of the population, the establishment of new industries or the decline of mineral working.
(ii) Changes that are bound to take place, but have not yet begun, for example, the results to be expected from dam or bridge construction that is already in progress.
(iii) Changes that ought to take place, though the conditions for them do not yet exist, such as improvement in the stock of houses, redevelopment of congested areas, etc.

In extreme cases (as noted in Chapter III "The Town in Relation to its Region") some physical obstacle may impose an absolute limit on the growth of the town, but this is very unusual. It would be truer to say that realistic consideration of the future of towns has often been hindered by sheer psychological inhibition, due to unwillingness to accept the present trend to urbanisation combined with irrational dislike of large towns. This has hindered recognition of how very large many towns are going to be, and thus distracted attention from the vital question of how to organise their growth efficiently.

In this stage of the report, therefore, it will be necessary to discuss a wide range of influences which make for growth or decline, with the aim of making a reasoned forecast of the size which the town should be expected to reach and the speed with which it should be expected to reach it. Of course, such forecasts cannot be precise, but it is very important to get the scale of thinking right and to understand the main factors influencing the speed of change.

Consideration should always be given to the scale of future migration from the rural areas around the town. In recent years rural migration has increased so much that many people fail to realise that it may yet increase much further. A big increase in migration must often be expected even though it is not easy to see how work will be found for all the migrants. Contrary to a widespread view, such migrants do not necessarily come to the town because they think that life there is going to be good, but because the prospects for them in the rural areas are so extremely bad as a result of the pressure of population on the land. Migration from rural areas may well prove to be one of the biggest influences on the future of the town and also one of the most difficult to cope with.

It is particularly important to be aware of possible *acceleration* in a town's growth, since expansion of certain services such as schools has to be begun several years before the extra places are needed.

Sometimes the most careful examination of future prospects may make it very difficult to decide what the future holds. Even in such a case, however, the work will not be wasted. At least it is then clear that one must organise on the basis of being ready for unexpected developments. Moreover, the main elements of uncertainty can probably be identified, so that one can see what new information would clear the air.

Comparative Rates of Growth. – The analysis should include a discussion of where the town now stands in the scale of towns in the region and where it is likely to stand in the future. As a centre, is it becoming of greater importance, or lesser? In the former case it may attract rural migration from a very wide area, including districts not within its normal sphere of influence. In the latter, much of the rural migration, even from the town's immediate neighbourhood, may go to other centres.

It is in connection with this issue that people who are disturbed by growth problems may put forward the idea of checking the town's growth. In particular, they may fear lack of employment for immigrants.

But it is virtually impossible to stop a town's growth by means of restrictions, which are usually the first remedy put forward. There is really only one way of stopping immigration and that is to make some other town more attractive to the migrants. If, therefore, further immigration to a town is considered to be absolutely catastrophic, owing to shortage of water, for example, the remedy must lie in action by the national government.

The conclusions on the growth of the town are likely to be highly qualified, but they should throw a good deal of light on at least the immediate future. There are three main possibilities.

(a) *Small Prospects of Growth.* – This may appear to present a simple problem, but it is not always so, because the town may need a good deal of improvement, such as the installation of modern services, while the financial resources are likely to be and to remain small.

(b) *Uncertain Prospects of Growth.* – This is likely to mean that the town's competitive position is itself uncertain, perhaps because some change in communications, such as a new road, is expected to benefit some other centre. It is rare, however, for uncertainty to threaten actual decline.

Sometimes uncertainty about future growth does not present special difficulties in preparing a town plan, because it is not immediately necessary to make crucial decisions, such as whether to develop a new and expensive source of water. Where such early decisions are required, the whole situation will probably need to be considered on a regional basis.

(c) *Prospects of Rapid Growth.* – This is the most likely situation in view of the present wave of urbanisation. Few town administrations are yet systematically organised to deal with growth and so even a moderate rate of growth is likely to prove uncomfortably fast.

4. *Problems of Development.* – These earlier sections of the report clear the stage for the main task of assessing the development problems and making recommendations for dealing with them. As usual, there are two aspects:

(i) adjusting the communal organisation to provide additional services at the requisite speed;
(ii) dealing with physical obstacles.

Even where the physical conditions are quite straightforward, the organisation of development requires considerable attention if the necessary work is to be executed efficiently and economically. This is a matter on which the town planner will be well advised to spend much time convincing the members of the town planning authority. The aim should be to start a regular building programme, so that extensions of public services can be carried out when they are required, instead of being hurriedly pushed through when they are overdue.

There is still a tendency to regard municipal expenditure as unproductive and therefore particularly suitable for being cut back in times of economic depression. Municipal expenditure, like all other economic activities, must certainly be subject to adjustment in time of crisis, but it is equally important that it should be accepted as a constant and increasing factor in the economy.

By this stage the report should have brought out the main facts relating to the town and their importance for the future. Some of these facts will speak for themselves. Statements as to the actual growth of population, the shift of population from one area to another, changes in industry and in flows of traffic should carry their own conviction. It should be recognised, however, that the lay reader, even when willing to accept the facts, will sometimes find difficulty in bearing them all in mind. That is one reason why it is important not to burden him with irrelevant material.

In the second place the report will have put forward deductions, which though important and probable, are impossible to prove beyond doubt. These will include such things as conclusions on future growth of population, on future trends in migration, on expected changes in road traffic, etc. Here the lay reader will have an involuntary tendency to dispute and reject those arguments which are least welcome because they raise difficulties. For this reason, even where the planner finds it necessary to adopt a relatively extreme forecast about some future movement, it may be useful for him to include a subsidiary argument as to the minimum movement *conceivable*. For example, if he feels that action should be based on the assumption that the annual population increase will be 5% (giving a total increase of over 50% in 10 years) he may find it useful to point out (i) that the annual natural increase by itself is over 2% and (ii) that recent increases from migration have been round about 3%. This would mean that, for the immediate future, an annual increase of less than 5% would involve a fall in *existing* trends.

Thirdly, the report will have outlined various problems without closely examining their character. Conflicts between different needs will have become evident, but the solution will not yet be clear.

In the remainder of the report the planner will have to explain what decisions need to be made, what conflicts must be resolved and must make suggestions as to how this should be done. For this purpose he must deal with complex relationships and will need to plan his argument carefully if the lay reader is not to become confused. (There is also a serious danger that the lay reader will put the whole document down in despair.)

In planning this last part of his report the planner will work it out much better if he distinguishes in his own mind the various types of relationship with which he must deal.

(a) Priorities and relative degrees of urgency.
(b) Logical interdependence. Some things cannot be done until others have been dealt with. A new site cannot be occupied until there is access to it.
(c) Duration in time. Some solutions are immediately available if there

is the will to use them. Others cannot be carried out quickly, particularly those which involve a good deal of construction.

(d) Resources. The planner must not make recommendations which ignore the availability of money, labour and materials. He may, of course, make recommendations to increase their availability.

Looking at the matter from another angle, the planner will find himself making recommendations of two kinds. For many purposes there will be no difficulty in deciding what should be done, but a good deal of care and trouble will be necessary to get it done efficiently. If a new residential area is to be opened up, arrangements will be needed to construct the main access, to build the subsidiary road network, to provide the main supplies and the subsidiary networks for all the services and to decide the type, density etc. of the dwellings, to ensure the due provision of schools, administrative services etc. Much of the actual work of doing all this will naturally fall to specialist departments concerned with different aspects of the municipal services, but their programmes of work must depend upon the town plan and the town plan must be influenced by what they can accomplish. The planner may therefore find himself closely concerned with matters quite outside the town such as the works necessary for the provision of a new source of water supply.

The second group of recommendations is that in which there is real difficulty in deciding what should be done, particularly where the decision is bound to have major effects on the way the town develops.

The future of the town centre is apt to be a particularly difficult problem. In many an old town it is evident that the town centre is more and more ceasing to be central because the town is developing in what one might loosely call a lopsided manner. This may be due to topographical difficulties, like the steep mountain on the eastern edge of Antakya in Turkey. At Cambridge, England, there is no real topographical difficulty, but the existence of many ancient and valued buildings makes further expansion of the existing centre extremely difficult and more or less forces the creation of a secondary centre. Port developments often have a big influence of this kind. At Marseilles in France, and at Bristol in England, changes in shipping techniques are steadily moving the centre of activity away from the old port in the centre of the town. At Cardiff, however, the declining importance of the docks has diminished the importance of the old business centre close to them. The most dramatic instance of change due to a port is perhaps Manchester, England, which in the last few years of the 19th century became a port, in spite of being an inland town, as a result of the building of a ship canal.

One of the most difficult of all town planning problems is the situation in which one or two necessary decisions are so farreaching that they must be decided in advance, as most of the plan depends upon them. Istanbul presents a striking example of how great the difficulties can be. It lies at the entrance to the Bosphorus and has always been notable for having relations with both Europe and Asia, as well as standing between the Black Sea and the Mediterranean. Istanbul always has been, and still is, an important port, but recent events have emphasised the importance of its land connections. This is partly a result of the development of the interior of Anatolia, which is now the heart of the political territory to which Istanbul belongs. Changes in transport techniques have had an influence in the same direction and one development of great significance is that in the technique of bridge building. Until recently it has been impossible to bridge the Bosphorus, and in consequence Istanbul has built up one of the biggest water transport commuting systems in the world. Nevertheless, the relative difficulty of transport to the Asiatic shore has continued to have a profound effect on the way in which the city develops. Now it has become possible to bridge the Bosphorus and the decision to do so has been taken. The most practicable sites for a bridge, however, are all to the north of the city, which might loosely be called also the "back" of the city, away from the hitherto dominant water front. The construction of a bridge is bound therefore to have a profound effect on the forces at work within the city, an effect so profound, in fact, that it is far from easy to see what the results will be.

This situation in Istanbul may be compared with that of Edinburgh, Scotland, where the recent construction of a road bridge across the River Forth has been a major improvement in transport *facilities*, but does not cause a comparable change in transport *routes*, since a considerable traffic across the Forth already took place by a ferry very close to the site of the new bridge.

Summary on Development Problems

The selection and ordering of the material for this last section of the report is accordingly a matter of great difficulty and it all too easily ends in a long list of detailed recommendations, in the course of which the lay reader rapidly loses his sense of what the individual proposals are. There is no simple answer to this problem, but the following points should be observed.

(i) As far as possible, each main problem should be handled as a whole, the detailed measures required for its solution being placed in appendices, the subject matter of each of which is clearly stated.
(ii) The plan of exposition and the reasons for it should be clearly stated, particularly if there is one problem which necessarily dominates

others, as the crossing of the Bosphorus must dominate any plan for Istanbul.

(iii) Constant care must be taken to keep all specific statements in context. It is important not to associate loosely two figures for expenditure which are essentially unlike, one perhaps being counterbalanced by expected revenue, while the other is not, or one being a major increase of expenditure under that head, while the other represents a mere continuance of the existing level of spending.

(iv) The drafting of the report should not be divorced from the arrangements for subsequent work. A complete summary of a town's development problems is necessarily difficult to absorb and care is needed to ensure that there are proper facilities for its digestion.

In connection with this last point, it may be useful to deal with the matter in stages by presenting some of the main studies before the complete and final conclusions are ready. This, however, easily produces an academic effect which does more harm than good. Both the town planning authority and the public at large easily get the impression that they are being presented with a piece of research remote from day-to-day problems, with which accordingly they do not bother much, if at all. This tendency to produce an impression of academic obscurity is one of the most serious sins to be laid at the door of town planners and is directly attributable to their failure to understand the conditions in which they necessarily work. That is to say that they fail to realise that they must seek to ensure that their work is widely understood. It is by no means necessary for this academic impression to be created, but it can only be avoided by taking constant trouble to emphasise and explain the practical issues.

The final result should be a report with the following characteristics.

(i) A clear plan clearly set out.

(ii) Simple exposition of the nature of each problem and of its significance.

(iii) Illustration by plans and statistical tables, each of which is clear in itself and plays a definite part in helping the reader. It is not enough to prepare a map showing certain necessary information. The map must bring out the important points clearly. It is salutary to run through all the illustrative material and ask oneself what the loss would be if part or the whole of each item were omitted. Only by some such rigorous check can one avoid burdening the reader with unnecessary material.

XVI

ACTION ON THE SYNTHESIS

One of the most serious defects of town planning has been the tendency for the whole movement to come to a halt once the presentation discussed in the previous chapter has been prepared and put forward. There are several reasons for this trouble and they are all relevant to finding a remedy.

The first trouble has been failure to regard town planning as a "process" at all, so that the town plan has sometimes been prepared without any regard to the problem of carrying it out or "implementing" it. Secondly, even if the planner recognises in theory the need for implementation, he may fail to take account of what it involves in practice, so that his final plan is not realistic and has not benefited from frequent and thorough consultation with the individuals and organisations on whom the task of implementation would fall, particularly the various municipal departments concerned with raising finance and executing works.

Thirdly, there has been no clear picture in anyone's mind of what series of actions implementation would involve, particularly if considered over a period of years.

Once the synthesis report has been completed and presented, further action falls into two main parts:

(i) getting the recommendations accepted by various bodies at various levels;
(ii) getting an executive programme started and keeping it going.

The first process, acceptance, is a complex matter and it is always to some extent qualified. The first need is to secure acceptance of the analysis of the problems, for there can obviously be no agreement on the recommendations unless there is a common view of the problems for which the recommendations are designed to be a remedy. For this purpose it is very important to present the facts purely as facts and not to mix the statement of them avoidably with allegations as to who has been responsible for creating the factual situation. This is perhaps a particular danger with regard to housing, in which there is much more likely to be agreement on the stark facts of the situation than on the question who is responsible for creating it. The actual shortage of good houses and extent of overcrowding need to be made clear, without arguing whether some particular malpractice has caused these deficiencies. The latter point will have to be pursued, but it should not be allowed to blur the facts.

If care is taken to separate the facts sufficiently rigorously and to set out clearly how they have been ascertained, there should be no serious difficulty in securing acceptance of the factual statement. The main difficulty is that the facts are usually inextricably interlocked with deductions, such as forecasts about the future course of population growth. However reasonable these deductions may be, they can never be fully proved to be correct at the time they are made and therefore offer more scope for objection by those to whom the conclusions in the forecasts are unwelcome. In such circumstances, however, it will often be possible to get agreement at least on the direction in which things will move, even if there is some conflict of view about the scale of the prospective movement, and this limited agreement is sometimes enough for immediate purposes.

To secure agreement about the recommendations is a much more difficult matter, and here one can distinguish several possible situations.

First, it will be appreciated that immediate agreement on all the recommendations is not necessary. In making the final presentation, therefore, care should be taken to make clear what decisions are required in order that useful work may proceed while the recommendations as a whole are further studied. Only very rarely will there be serious difficulty about getting agreement on a preliminary short programme.

Secondly, one can distinguish the points on which there is a partial disagreement, for example, as to the scale of action required, rather than a desire positively to reject a particular solution. For example, if the presentation is based on the view that the population of the town, at present 50,000, will grow to 200,000 by the end of the century, difficulty may be found in securing acceptance of this high rate of growth. If, however, objectors can be brought to accept that such a high rate of growth is at least a possibility, and that therefore no action should be taken which would be incompatible with it, the worst difficulties can be avoided and in the next few years the facts of growth may spread conviction that a very high rate of growth has got to be faced.

The real trouble arises when there is fundamental disagreement on a cardinal point, so that if the recommendation is not accepted the whole basis of the presentation would have to be altered. A crisis of this kind could arise at Istanbul if, after a plan has been prepared incorporating a bridge over the Bosphorus, the Government were to decide after all that a bridge was impracticable and that crossing should continue indefinitely to take place by ferry. The elimination of the bridge would radically alter several principal features of the plan. A trouble somewhat of this kind has in fact existed at Kingston-upon-Hull in England where one of the big issues is the construction of a bridge over the estuary of the Humber. As the main existing connections of the city were along the river, rather than across it, the positive necessity of building a bridge was for many years difficult to demonstrate, while there were at least three other estuarial crossings in Great Britain where bridges or tunnels could be held to be of more immediate importance.

This particular difficulty is specially liable to arise where the only really effective solution is a very expensive one, so expensive perhaps, that the decision can only be taken at the national level. This may also be necessary where the local people are either unable to agree or unwilling to take a highly unpopular decision. In England at both Oxford and Cambridge it has proved impossible to find a scheme for reorganising the old and congested centre of the town which is not highly controversial, and the ultimate solution will probably require the exercise of national authority.

In such highly controversial situations time is always required for the achievement of a satisfactory settlement, but time alone will be useless unless a *progressive discussion* can be instituted. This is one of the crucial and still largely unsolved problems of modern town planning, for progress in such cases nearly always depends upon the discussion by a large number of people of what one might call a complex of points, associated with each other in an intricate way. This is a very difficult kind of discussion to maintain, even between a few people, and when many people are involved some of them always seek to oversimplify the issues. Then it is easy for a public outcry to arise which is based on a misunderstanding of what is at stake.

There is no easy solution to this problem, but a condition of any solution is that the importance of the matter should be thoroughly understood and that the discussions should be planned with great care. (See also Chapter VI pp. 55-56 "The Town Planner's Relations with the lic".)

Assuming, however, that a substantial area of agreement is achieved, work can proceed within that area and the next task is to prepare an executive programme. This involves agreed measures in several different fields, and the steps may be outlined as follows.

(a) A decision must be arrived at as to the nature and extent of the private development to be expected over a given period, since this will be the main determinant of the amount of public development (services etc.) which will be required. In addition, account must be taken of other forms of public development, such as the erection of a hospital or a military depot.

(b) The needs resulting from (a) will, of course, be discussed with the various organisations responsible for the execution of work and must then be analysed and qualified, so that priorities, durations and costs can all be determined. These must then be compared with the availability of labour, materials and finance. If, as may well be the case, the existing supplies prove inadequate, consideration must be given to expanding the supply, which always requires time, apart from any other difficulties.

The result should be a detailed programme for the immediate future which will cause a certain amount of work to be carried out for the implementation of the plan. Any such first programme will need to be followed by a series of further ones. A large part of these programmes will consist of routine work that the various municipal departments would in any event have carried out, but careful programming will ensure that the work is systematised and the available resources are spread as scientifically as possible over the field in the light of the various needs.

This is all that is required to get the work started, but it is of course necessary to ensure that the volume of the work is sufficient to meet the needs of the town's growth and change on a long-term basis. This is a much more difficult task because, as we have noted repeatedly, at present few societies are organised on a basis which permits sufficient resources to be devoted to municipal matters. It is not merely a question of the community recognising its problems and developing the will to solve them. In addition, considerable ingenuity is required to develop the necessary organisation and also the necessary attitudes of mind, so that men can learn to understand much more fully what living in towns involves.

If the work is successfully developed on the lines sketched above, a new *esprit de corps* will be developed. All those concerned with the management of the town will recognise (i) the basic facts, (ii) the nature of the problems, (iii) what is required for action on them, (iv) the extent of the progress made at any one moment, (v) the adequacy or inadequacy of this result in the light of the problems to come. Then, and then only, will a proper basis have been laid for efficient town management.

All might then seem well, or on the way to being so, but one further warning should be uttered. It is just when one feels that the problems have been mastered (whatever the field of work) that the whole situation is apt to take an unexpected turn, so that one finds oneself facing new problems, as yet unexplored. Constant alertness is therefore necessary, but the most unexpected turn of events will be easier to deal with once a team is in being which is dedicated to meeting and solving town management problems.

FURTHER READING

This further reading list is quite short because an effort has been made to limit it to books which are reasonably easy to appreciate without an intimate knowledge of the country about which they are written. Articles have been excluded, partly because each usually covers only a small amount of ground and also because they are often not readily available except where there are extensive libraries.

Chapter I: Town and Regional Planning

The reader who wishes to gain a fuller idea of national or regional planning can perhaps best do so by looking at:
(i) A national plan for a small country. This can give a good idea of the ground covered without being too bulky or complex. For example, *Third Programme: Social and Economic Development 1969-72* (Government Publications Sales Office, Dublin, Ireland).

(ii) Published regional planning reports such as those for the English regions, for example, *The West Midlands* (H.M.S.O., London, 1965); or O.E.C.D., *Report on the Planning of Thrace in Turkey* (Paris, 1968).

Chapter II: The Present-Day Importance of Towns

Almost any general book on town planning or on urban economics will include a passage about the present wave of urbanisation, but in order to go deeper into the subject it is necessary to study the process of urbanisation in particular countries. Unfortunately, there is little penetrating work on this, particularly work of a comparative nature.

Peter Hall's *World Cities* (Weidenfeld & Nicolson, England, World University Library, paperback, 1966) describes seven metropolitan cities and their recent evolution, but it should not be taken as a sound guide to other big conurbations.

As far as smaller towns are concerned, there is little which is easy for a general reader not intimately acquainted with the country concerned. However, it can be quite useful to read a regional report which covers a suitably varied selection of towns.

Chapter III: The Town in Relation to its Region

Here again the best approach is to study good regional reports since these are always concerned with the relations between the towns in the region.

There have also been good studies for the expansion of certain towns in Britain which incidentally give a good idea of the background of the town concerned.

Chapter IV: Notes on Metropolitan Areas and Decentralisation

See Peter Hall's *World Cities* referred to under Chapter II. A valuable study on Calcutta, *Basic Development Plan, Calcutta Metropolitan District 1966-86*, was published by the Calcutta Metropolitan Planning Organisation, Development and Planning Department, Government of West Bengal, in 1966, but it is arguable that in some respects Calcutta is a rather special case.

The Regional City: an Anglo-American Discussion on Metropolitan Planning, edited by Derek Senior (Longman's, London, 1966), is interesting on one of the current theories about metropolitan areas, but as it discusses only Britain and America it may mislead students from other countries.

Books that were once famous, such as two reports on Greater London prepared by Professor Abercrombie at the end of World War II, are now too old to be a sound guide for the study of current problems.

Chapter V: New Towns

It is difficult to find good critical work on the advantages and problems of new towns generally. *British New Towns* by Lloyd Rodwin deals only with the early stages of the British new town movement.

Hook New Town (Greater London Council, 1965) describes the preparatory studies for a new town project in England which in the end was not carried out.

A good deal of comment on new towns, for example on Chandighar in India, is devoted mainly to the town as an example of civic design and lay-out and does not go into the problems of justification or economic success.

Chapter VI: A Town Planner's Approach to his Problem

The author knows of no book which approaches the subject in quite the same way as this chapter, but Brian J. McLoughlin's *Urban and Regional*

Planning: A Systems Approach (Faber, London, 1969) contains valuable material on the kind of thinking involved, though it presupposes a more sophisticated organisation and a greater availability of statistical material than it has been thought right to assume in this book. Unlike many general handbooks on town planning it is not written mainly in terms of circumstances and institutions of one country.

Lewis Keeble's *Principles and Practice of Town and Country Planning* (4th edition, The Estates Gazette Ltd., London, 1969) has the advantage of showing a healthy scepticism about certain fashions in planning. Its background is British.

Chapter VII: Town Planning and the Law

As far as the author is aware, all handbooks on town planning law relate to the law of a particular country only and thus are of limited value in illustrating the basic principles.

Chapter VIII: The Characteristics of Private Development

Here again, the difficulty is that all detailed studies are heavily influenced by the circumstances of a particular country. Moreover, the situation in any one country can change pretty rapidly if capital for urban building becomes more readily available. Books about Britain are only partially applicable even to countries as close as Ireland and can be seriously misleading as a clue to conditions in, say, Sweden, not to speak of countries further afield.

Chapter IX: Growth and Change in Towns

The difficulty here is that much urban history, however interesting, is not relevant to current problems, which vary greatly according to the country concerned. *The Towns of Ghana: The Role of Service Centres in Regional Planning* by D. Grove and L. Huszar (Ghana University Press, Accra, 1964) is an interesting study of the emergence of a new town pattern as the result of changing conditions.

Chapter X: Internal Improvements

Few books have been written on the principles of this, and individual improvement schemes, even when fully documented, are very difficult to study without an intimate study of the town concerned.

Bei Fragen zur Produktsicherheit wenden Sie sich bitte an:
If you have any questions regarding product safety,
please contact:

Walter de Gruyter GmbH
Genthiner Straße 13
10785 Berlin
productsafety@degruyterbrill.com